CodeWell Academy()

and

R.M.Z. Trigo

present:

# Programming Swift,
## Master's Handbook
## Edition
## *Code like a PRO in 24 hrs or less!*
*Proven Strategies & Process!*
*A Beginner's TRUE guide to Code,*
*with Data Structures & Algorithms*


## *Master's Handbook Series*

# Table of Contents

# Introduction

===========================  ======

## Welcome to the Path of Mastery

We thank you for purchasing & downloading our work, the Master's Handbook. By doing so, we can tell you have a curiosity to learn Programming in a deeper, more comprehensive way.

We notice that you don't just want to learn a few tricks here and there, but you want the confidence to take on any programming challenge with ease.

Hence, you've come to the right place...

## The Master's Circle

You aren't alone.

Behind this book are programmers hailing from some of the most Best Computer Science Programs taught by some of the most Advanced Universities in the World Today.

## Foundations

There are two major things that you need to do to be a good programmer. One is to get a good amount of practice. The other is to get a really good education.

But how can you tell what source of education is good or not?

You see, we can tell you that 90% of programming learning sources out there will show you WHAT the code is and HOW it works, for any amount of Programming languages. But that's not necessarily a bad thing - and plenty of those sources are really good too.

However, they might not teach you WHY or WHEN you would use that code. NOR would they show you WHAT ELSE you might need with that code.

If you needed to program something, you don't want to be someone that knows a bunch of code but with no real idea how to use them, right?

As you read on, you'll quickly learn not just the HOW and WHAT the code is, but the WHERE, WHEN,

WHY to use it, WHAT ELSE you'll need with it- and more importantly, HOW to use it.

**The Master Structure**

We start by observing the world and defining the code to represent things (data) or actions (functions). As you progress through the book, you'll find more advanced concepts and ways to combine them all together.

You're also accommodated with the Main Programming Language this book comes with, as well as general PseudoCode to help understand coding concepts. Often times, you'll find that our PseudoCode bridges you from learning this Book's Main Language to learning your Next Language!

Whether you haven't coded a single line before, or you've already build serious projects, you WILL find great value in this book. Often times, you'll run into a coding challenge in your programming journey. This book will help you identify how to progress through it!

========================= ======

# Editor's Note

========================== ======

**Reality**

If you ever wonder why Computer Scientists make so much money (including junior programmers, developers, software engineers, IT folks, and just about any job involving programming), there are plenty of good reasons.

One, is that in today's world, just about EVERY industry out there requires a level of technological sophistication. So you can imagine the level of demand for a qualified programmer.

But the truth about Computer Science is that it can be very intellectually challenging most of the time. Thus, only a certain number of people will be good enough to get a real career in programming.

So there you have it. High Demand + Few Good Programmers = GOOD Salary.

However, you may not need a university degree to be a good programmer...

## In-Depth

The true point of this book, along with others in the series, is to go deeper than the lines of code you see. You'll learn how to use every bit of data and code to any situation you encounter - and at one point, intuitively.

A real programmer's job is to create tools that improve life in one way or another. Almost all of the time, it will involve having to come up with ways to represent things in life as data - as well as getting a computer to process the data properly and turn into something useful.

So if you want to become a better programmer, read on...

# SWIFT Introduction

**SWIFT: " Here's to the Crazy Ones... "**

In the summer of 2014, Apple unveiled a New, Unique Programming Language for all future Apple products and Technologies. This language is called Swift.

And rightly so, Swift does live up to its name. As you'll learn later, the Swift Language has support for static data - meaning that programs can run much faster when their data is much more easily accessible. Also, the Swift syntax is beautifully designed. It's a great entry-point for most beginner programmers, as the language is quite easy and quick to learn.

As you can imagine, the Swift language is limited within Apple hardware & software only. However, due to the flexibility, speed, and strengths borrowed from other great programming languages, the Swift language may be the ONLY language needed for Apple.

Even if the Swift language hasn't quite had it's time to age yet, you can imagine how many skilled Swift programmers will soon emerge as the years go by. Just stay tuned.

## SWIFT Advantages:

- higher performance

- data flexibility

- more friendly and concise syntax

- beginner-friendly

- uses the strengths of other great programming languages (i.e. C++. PHP, Ruby, Python...)

## SWIFT Disadvantages:

- Applies to Apple Hardware/Software Only! (OSX or iOS)

- New programming language = less support & talented developers

**SWIFT Workshops:**

These workshops are yours to complete in whichever way you like (However, the code MUST work!).

They're designed to put the most recent concepts into real-life practice, yet giving you the flexibility and critical thinking along the way.

And of course, flexibility and deep critical thinking are key programmer traits!

Find them throughout the book!

========================= ======

# Prelude: Atomic Data Types

First off, we'll briefly start with primitive data types. It's important to know what they are, because you'll be identifying real-life information with them later.

## Booleans

Booleans, often called bools, are either TRUE or FALSE. This is the simplest data type, but often one of the most important. A LOT of functionality depends on Booleans, as you will find out later

A Boolean will always be a two-state situation. For example, the lights in your living room are either on (TRUE) or off (FALSE).

## Integers

These are all the standard whole numbers, both positive and negative. The highest and lowest integers depend on the number of bits to represent them (i.e. 8-bit integers, 16-bit, etc.). Mathematic and boolean operators often use Integers,.i.e.

*10 + 50 == 60,*

*-4 - 12, != -10,*

and so on.

## Characters

These are all letters and symbols that can be represented by ASCII characters. Think of one character as a single symbol or letter.

## Floats

Formally called floating-point numbers, these represent decimals - including the decimal point and decimal numbers beyond.

Examples:

*2.3*

*0.75*

# Prelude: Data Sequences & Combinations

## Strings

These are merely a collection of Characters in sequence. Think of these as words or phrases.

In most programming languages, Strings are represented by a sequence of characters between quotation marks: *"Hi there"*, or *"Hello."*, for example.

How these would look like as a sequence of characters is as follows:

*"Hi There"* is represented as characters H,i, space, T, h,e , r, and e

*"Hello."* is represented as characters H, e, l, l, o, and the period.

## Lists

These are a sequence of individual elements put together as a list. Often times, all the elements within that list are the same data type

Examples would be:

a List of Integers: *[3, 1, 4, 9, 2]*

a List of Strings: *["Apple", "Banana", "Caramel"]*

a List of Booleans: *[true, false, true, true]*

**Enumerations**

These are fixed sets of data values. The data within these sets are the same data type. You would have to choose between one of the data elements within that set.

For example, traffic lights are either red, orange, or green.

As an enumeration, traffic lights would be: *["Red, "Green", "Yellow"]*

What differs Enumerations from lists is that Enumerations have a FIXED set of values. You wont be able to add or delete the elements unless you edit the code directly.

**Itemizations**

Itemizations combine different data types together to form a finite set. Depending on the data type of a single element, you'll have to process that data in a certain way (you'll learn about this later in function templates).

Enumerations have the same data type, but Itemizations have different data types in the set. You also won't be able to add or delete any of the elements as well.

For example, a Space Rocket launch would be a set of integers 10 to 1, then the booleans true or false, to signifiy whether or not it has launched yet.

As an itemization, a Space Rocket Launch would be: [ false, 10, 9, ... 1, true]

# Prelude: Your Coding Environment

### Simple Online IDE

For now, it's all about understanding all the Programming Concepts, from the simple to the downright advanced.

To test out these concepts, you'll only need a simple online Compiler to run your code and make sure it works the way you planned it to.

Here's one online. It's FREE and it doesn't require any membership to test out your code:

www.swiftstub.com

### Full Development Kits

You may also set up your computer for app development, if you wish.

First, identify what Programming Language(s) and Framework(s) you wish to use. Then choose and set up the ideal Integrated Development Environment (IDE) for your language-framework combinations.

Popular IDE's include IntelliJ, Eclipse, Netbeans, CodeLite, XCode (for Mac Users) and more. But remember: make sure your IDE supports the programming languages of your choice.

# NOTE: Comments

For those only learning how to program, it's important to describe what your lines of code are and why you have them.

For programming teams, comments are essential. Even seasoned programmers who work in teams need to explain what their code does and why they have it. They find that it saves them time in analyzing and figuring out other people's code. They will also have less errors along the way - knowing that they're coding what they mean to, or editing code to be the way they originally want it to be.

# PART I: Your Code Structure and Foundations

# Chapter 1: Defining & Designing your Data

Anything in this universe can be represented by data. Your name, age, gender, what car you drive, what city you live in, country, planet, galaxy, and so on.

To design great apps, games, and any other digital tool you can think of, you'll have to identify what type of data you're dealing with.

**Identify your Data Type**

There are two questions to ask yourself when you're designing data to represent something.

First, identify whether or not you can define that 'thing' as an Integer, Number, Boolean (yes/no type things), or String. For example, your name is a String (a sequence of letters), your Age is a Number, and you live in a City or Town. Your city of town has a name - another String.

Second, identify whether or not that thing is a part of a whole; included in a larger thing. For example, you may have a friend named Jamie. She's included in a list of your friends.

## Representing your information as a Data Type

In most programming languages, you can define your data in a line of code. Here we define your data as a Global Variable - meaning this editable line of data is available throughout your program.

In most languages, you'll very likely declare the Type of data you represent, as well as the Name of your data.

Let's start with your name, using pseudocode for now:

*String NAME;*

In the above line of code, you defined your data as a String of characters, labelled as a NAME.

## An Explanation for your Data

A good practice in defining your data is to make comments above the line of code that explains why you have your data the way it is. One of the lines can be in the format of "_____ is a (Data Type)".

In most programming languages, comments usually start with two slashes (//). For the pseudocode we use here, we'll do the same

For the above line, here's the example:

*// My Name is a String*
*String NAME;*

Here are some more examples:

*// My Age is a Number*
*Number AGE;*
*// I live in a City or Town, with a Name*
*// My city's name is a String*
*String CITY;*
*// I am either hungry or not*
*// My hunger status is a Boolean*
*Boolean HUNGRY?;*
*// I either have a pet or I don't*
*// Whether or not I have a pet is a Boolean*
*Boolean HASPET?;*

# SWIFT-01: Defining & Designing your Data

## SWIFT Comments

In Swift, comments are just the same as other common languages like Java, C, C++, PHP, and even our own pseudocode.

Single-line comments start with two slashes (//) and end when the line breaks to the next line of code.

Multiple comment lines start with a slash and a star (/*) and end with the reverse: a star and a slash (*/). Often, multiple comment lines also start with stars (*) on each line.

Here's an example:

```
/* This is a
* multi-line
* comment */
```

## Atomic Data in SWIFT

Booleans are all in lowercase letters (true, false). If your booleans have any uppercase letters in them (True, TRUE), your code won't work.

Floats need to have the Zero (0) and the Decimal point. For example, 0.21 can be a float in Swift, but not .21.

Other than this, most atomic data in Swift have the same syntax as the ones from the Prelude.

**SWIFT Data Definitions**

The beautiful thing about defining data in Swift is how closely it can resemble an actual speaking language.

Do you remember high school math classes? When the textbooks had to assign variables like x and y, they would be something that resembles "let x = 12, or let y = 200".

In Swift, it works just the same way:

let (Variable Name) = (Initial Value)

It's simply like our pseudocode, but we add the word 'let' before the variable name.

In Swift, you don't need to declare the data types for your variables. However, you have to initialize your data once you define it.

However, compared to other languages such as Java, C, C++, and PHP, you don't need semicolons (;) at the end of your lines.

So let's Practice. Let's define the data for your friend's name. Let's call her Serena.

First, add a comment to take note of what data type you need:

// Serena's name is a String

Then let's define her name's data.

*// Katie's name is a String*
*let NAME = "Serena"*

Once you compile your code, your variable NAME will be a String, since you've initially set NAME using a string.

**PRACTICE:**

Let's start by declaring things that follow into each of: Strings, Numbers, Integers, and Booleans.

Fill in the blanks below, and copy-paste code between the lines to an IDE of your choice. If you use a Mac computer, Xcode is an ideal IDE for the Swift language.

You may also use online IDE's such as swiftstub.com,

```
// ————————————

// Joyce's name is a _____
let HERNAME = "_____"
// Joyce's age  is a ____
let HERAGE = _
// Joyce is either Married or not.
// Joyce's Marriage Status is a ___
let ISSHEMARRIED = _

println(HERNAME)
println(HERAGE)
```

*println("Is Joyce Married?")*
*println(ISSHEMARRIED)*

*// ————————————*

If you try to run your code - and it runs correctly - you should see the following:

Joyce

(whatever you set her age to)

(true or false, whatever you set it to)

# Chapter 2: Compound/Composite Data

From the last chapter's example, you can start to wonder that there just has to be a way to group all that data: your name, age, location, whether or not you have pets, etc.

Also, notice that a person can neither be a String, Number, Integer, nor Boolean. A person just holds too much data to be defined as either one of the above.

So what do we do?

## What a Composite Data Structure is

From the previous example, you can think of all the data you've defined as small parts of a whole. But what is this "whole"?

Enter Composite Data.

A Composite Data structure includes many parts of data within it.

Those parts of the Composite could be whatever you wish to declare. Strings, Integers, Booleans, Lists, and even Other Composite Data.

## Identify & Defining a Composite Data Structure

When you were asked earlier to define what type of data are you dealing with, what if you designed & defined data for an object that you couldn't identify as atomic data? What if it had plenty of Characteristics? What if there was more depth in that object?

The key thing to remember in identifying composite data is depth. There are more parts to that 'thing' you were trying to define as data. If there's more to anything than just a name, number, or true/false switch, then it's probably going to be a composite data structure.

### Representing information as Composite Data

Let's take YOU as an example. You are a Person. As a person, you're not JUST a name or number; you are comprised of a lot of data. An endless amount of data, rather.

## The Elements that Comprise your Data

As an example of Composite Data, let's define you.

For now, let's start with the basics.

Remember: you are a Person. Using simple pseudocode, let's define that:

```
//  I am a PERSON
CompositeStructure PERSON;
```

## An Explanation for your Composite Data's Parts

Similar to what you did earlier for defining data, it's also best that you identify what your composite data structure is comprised of.

For practice, use comments to describe what your data structure has.

Following the example above, You have a Name and an Age as well. Let's include that:

```
//  I am a PERSON
// A person has:
// - a name (string)
// - an age (number)
CompositeStructure Person {
String NAME;
Number AGE;
{
```

You live in a City. Oh but wait, a City isn't just a name is it? It's comprised of plenty of data as well!

```
//  This is a CITY
// A City has:
// - a name (string)
// - a Latitude and Longitude (2 numbers)
// - a Population count (an integer, above 0)
CompositeStructure City {
String NAME;
Number LATITUDE;
Number LONGITUDE;
Integer POPULATION;
{
```

Let's not forget about YOU now. You live in a City, remember?

```
//  I am a PERSON
// A person has:
// - a name (string)
// - an age (number)
// - a City they live in (Composite data City)
CompositeStructure PERSON {
String NAME;
Number AGE;
City LOCATION;
}
```

Notice what happened here. A compound data structure within another compound data structure!

# Chapter 3: Data Initialization

Let's recall the Composite Data Structure of a Person:

*// A person has:*
*// - a name (string)*
*// - an age (number)*
*// - a City they live in (Composite data City)*
*CompositeStructure PERSON {*
*String NAME;*
*Number AGE;*
*City LOCATION;*
*}*

*We'll also create two Atomic Data pieces as the Time: two integers.*

*Integer HOUR;*
*Integer MINUTE;*

You have have noticed one thing: You've defined what types of data you're dealing with - but we don't know any people yet. Nor do we know what time it is!

Now we INITIALIZE our data. Now that we've defined what types of data we have, we then set our data for the first time.

## Initializing Atomic Data

First, we'll set the time.
Let's say it's 8:30 PM. We'll set up our time as is.

To set data, most programming languages use the Equals (=) operator. Here, we'll do the same.

HOUR = 20;
MINUTE = 30;

**DON'T make this mistake...**

But what if we tried to set HOUR and MINUTE to another data type?

HOUR = aaaa;
MINUTE = Composite{Integer; String; Boolean} ;

Notice earlier that you've set both HOUR and MINUTE as Integers. Here, we're trying to set up those data as different data types. In some programming languages, it's not going to work. And in most cases, your code might not work because of this.

Here, you've set up your data as Integers - therefore, you need to initialize & change them as Integers.

Lesson learned: if you set up your data as a certain data type, unless you really know what you're doing, DO NOT try to set up that data as another data type!

**Initializing Composite Data Structures**

Now, let's define an actual Person using our data structure.
There are FOUR KEY steps to do this:

STEP ONE:
Identify & describe a data object you're trying to create.
For practice, use comments to describe what that object is & what it's like.
We'll use a friend of yours called Jamie, for example. We use comments to describe her:

*// Jamie Denise is a person*
*// She has:*
*// - a name: Jamie Denise*
*// - an age: 19*
*// - a City she lives in: New York*

STEP TWO:
Declare what type of composite data your object is.
In this example, we declare Jamie as a person:

*// Jamie Denise is a person*
*Person Jamie;*

STEP THREE:
You INITIALIZE your object's data structure, so that your object actually IS represented by the Composite Data in your program. In most languages, you declare that you have a new 'case' or instance of this object. Think of this step as "registering" your new object into your data program.

In this example, we INITIALIZE Jamie as a data object that HAS the Person Composite Data Structure

*// Jamie Denise is a person*
*Person Jamie = new Person;*
Again, just like Atomic Data, we use the Equals (=) operator to set data.

STEP FOUR:
Identify your object. Then, for each data part that your Composite Data is made of, set those initial values.

Remember Jamie's Attributes?

*// Jamie Denise is a person*
*// She has:*
*// - a name: Jamie Denise*
*// - an age: 19*
*// - a City she lives in: New York*

Now let's initialize each attribute onto our Data Object Jamie. You first need to identify the data object you're trying to reach. In this case, it's Jamie. Next (and this is important!), identify which attribute you're planning to reach. Here's it's best to reference the Data Structure you've defined earlier:

*CompositeStructure PERSON {*
*String NAME;*
*Number AGE;*
*City LOCATION;*
*}*

Let's set all three of Jamie's Attributes:

*// Jamie Denise is a person*

```
// She has:
// - a name: Jamie Denise
// - an age: 19
// - a City she lives in: New York
Person Jamie = new Person;
Jamie-NAME = "Jamie";          // <— a "String":
Remember?
Jamie-AGE = Nineteen;
CITY = NewYork;
```

Okay, we're done.
Hold on. This code is wrong. Why?

**DON'T make these mistakes...**

This line: *Jamie-AGE = Nineteen;* won't work. Why?
Just a friendly reminder. Make sure the data type you're trying to set MATCHES the data type you've defined. In most programming languages, this is one of the most common mistakes programmers make. Nineteen is definitely not a Number data type, nor is it a String (where's the "Quotation marks?"). However, 19 works.

*Jamie-AGE = 19;*

Also, This line: *CITY = NewYork;* won't work. Why?
What's CITY? Did we mean Jamie's current CITY? Remember to first identify the DATA OBJECT you're accessing. AND THEN that object's attributes.
Well, let's try that.

*Jamie-CITY = NewYork;*

This line: *Jamie-CITY = NewYork;* won't work either. Why?

Because Jamie is a data object that follows the Person Composite Data Structure you've defined. And note how that Structure does NOT have any attributes named CITY in it.

Again, Remember to first identify the DATA OBJECT you're accessing. AND THEN access that object's correct attributes.

The Person Structure includes a separate City data structure, but it certainly isn't called CITY.

```
CompositeStructure PERSON {
String NAME;
Number AGE;
City LOCATION;
}
```

Oh, so it should be *Jamie-LOCATION= NewYork;*

But you're missing one more thing. Where in your program is NewYork defined?

Well, that can be arranged. Let's recall the City data Structure and define the NewYork data object as well:

```
// This is a CITY
// A City has:
// - a name (string)
// - a Latitude and Longitude (2 numbers)
// - a Population count (an integer, above 0)
CompositeStructure City {
String NAME;
Number LATITUDE;
```

*Number LONGITUDE;*
*Integer POPULATION;*
*{*


*//  NewYork is a CITY*
*// NewYork has:*
*// - a name: "New York"*
*// - a Latitude and Longitude: 40.7127 and 74.0059*
*// - a Population count: 8406000*
*City NewYork = new City;*
*NewYork-NAME = "New York";*
*NewYork-LATITUDE = 40.7127;*
*NewYork-LONGITUDE = 74.0059;*
*NewYork-POPULATION = 8406000;*


and now, we fully complete Jamie's data entry:

*// Jamie Denise is a person*
*// She has:*
*// - a name: Jamie Denise*
*// - an age: 19*
*// - a City she lives in: New York*
*Person Jamie = new Person;*
*Jamie-NAME = "Jamie";*
*Jamie-AGE = 19;*
*Jamie-LOCATION= NewYork*

# SWIFT-02: Compound/Composite Data

Swift is an Object-Oriented Programming language, meaning that the code revolves around Composite Data Structures called Classes. Once the code is run, the computer creates Data Objects based on the Classes you've designed with your code.

Think of Classes as Blueprints for a house, and Objects as actual houses designed from the Blueprints.

And since Swift is an Object-Oriented language, Class attributes or variables may also be referred to as Fields.

### Data Structures and Data Classes in SWIFT

In Swift, you can design both data classes and data structures - called Structs.

However, there are differences in choosing either one to design your data. Classes in Swift, in general, allow for far more flexibility in creating and changing your data. Plus, data classes in Swift allow for far more flexibility in terms of Memory Management. Meanwhile, structs in Swift are generally quicker to load and access. Computer hardware and Memory Management will all covered in another work. Stay tuned!

**Creating a Class or Data Structure in SWIFT**

First, classes in Swift always start with the word class, then the class name, then curly brackets containing all code within the class

Same idea for structs. The word struct, the struct name, then code within curly brackets.

Overall, typical Composite Data classes or structs in Swift looks like this:

```
class ClassName {
        // insert code here
}
struct StructName {
        // insert code here
}
```

## Class and Struct Variables in Swift

In Swift, variables within structs and classes are defined and initialized nearly the same way as our Pseudocode. Except for one difference: you add the word 'var' just before the variable name.

So if you added attributes to the above classes, they would look like so:

```
class ClassName {
    let attribute1 = "string"
    let attribute2 = 123
}
struct StructName {
    let attribute1 = true
    let attribute2 = 0.123
}
```

## Optional Variables

In Swift, there are variables that can be defined, but don't require any initial value. These are called Optional Variables. However, you DO need to assign what data type, class, or struct that the variable will have. It also follows a different syntax compared to assigning a usual variable.

Within a class or struct, you can assign optional variables like so:

*let variableName: <datatype>?*

So for example, we can add this line to either one of the data structures above:

*let attribute3: String?*

Afterwards, attribute3 can either be a String or a null value (nothing).

**Initializing a Swift Struct or Class**

To create an Object based on your class, it's as if you were setting a variable (i.e. variablename = initialvalue).

However, you would assign that variable as your class. You would do this by using your defined class name, then a set of Parentheses '()'

For example, you would initialize your classes and structs like so:

*let struct = StructName()*
*let class = ClassName()*

**Accessing Class Attributes**

This follows a similar structure to our PseudoCode.

To access a Class Attribute, you first have an object that has been assigned that Class structure. Then follow it up with a period (.) and the class attribute you want to access.

Let's recall setting object1 into a class:

let object1 = ClassName()

Then accessing object1's attributes would look like the following notation:

object1.attribute1

Can you guess what data type you end up with when you access these two class attributes? If you look at your data definition for your Class, you've defined the attributes for that class with specific data types. Therefore:

object1.attribute1 (this returns a String, since you've set it as one)

object1.attribute2 (this returns an Integer, since you've set it as one)

# SWIFT Workshop #1

Now we'll be putting what you've learned so far into practice.

If you use a Mac computer, Xcode is an ideal IDE for the Swift language.

You may also use online IDE's such as swiftstub.com,

## Two Cups of Coffee

Let's start defining Composite Data Structures. We will use both Structs and Classes to give you an idea of what situations you would use them in.

Now think of two different cups of coffee. One cup is readily accessible in your kitchen, but it will be a certain brand, flavour, and cup size. The other cup can become any brand, flavour, and size you want. However, you can only acquire it from the famous coffee shop two blocks from your house.

Before we get started, let's use comments to describe what our our data will look like.

```
/*
The 1st CoffeeCup Has:
*/
/*
The 2nd CoffeeCup Has:
*/
```

Of course, one cup is a Struct and the other is a Class. Can you guess which one?

Yes, the Coffee Cup from your house is the Struct and the one from the coffee shop is the Class.

The rule of thumb is: if you want something quick and simple, design a Struct. If you want flexibility, design a Class.

Now think of the attributes both cups of coffee have.

Your home-brewed Coffee probably has a coffee brand, but you're stuck with what it is. It also has a flavour and a cup size, but you're stuck with what's there as well:

```
/*
* The Home-Brewed Coffee Cup Has:
* - a coffee brand
```

```
* - a flavour
* - a cup size
*/
```

Now, let's design your Home-Brew. Keep in mind that it is a Struct! For now, just initialize the values as such; you will have to change them during instances anyway.

```
struct HomeBrewCoffee {
    var brand = "Starbucks
    var flavor = "Home-brew Pike Place Roast"
    var cupSize = "Mug"
}
```

Next, your store-bought coffee definitely has a coffee brand. It also has a flavour, cup size, price, coffee condiments, and more.

```
/*
* The Coffee Shop Cup Has:
* - a coffee brand
* - a flavour
* - a cup size
* - a price
* - coffee condiments
*/
```

Now, let's design your Coffee Shop Brew. Keep in mind that it is a Class! Again, just initialize the values as such.

```
class CoffeeShopCoffee {
    var brand = ""
    var flavor = ""
    var cupSize = ""
    var price = ""
    var condiments:String?
}
```

## Playing with your Coffee

First, make sure to have BOTH the CoffeeShopCoffee class and HomeBrewCoffee struct in your code.

Now define two data definitions called 1stCoffee and 2ndCoffee. Set one variable to your class and the other to your struct.

Now, explore the differences between the two composite data types. If you can (or if you've read ahead), create subclasses of the original class. Compare accessing speeds if you know how.

# Chapter 4: Data Changes &

# Mutable States

In the previous chapters, you've defined some facts as data structures and even represented people and cities as data.

However, nothing ever stays the same in data.

Data changes over time - and it's important to keep track of how data values change and what they currently are.

## Modifying your Defined Data Over Time

In reality, modifying the data values you've set in place is nearly similar to initializing them in the first place. In most programming languages, the same principles between initializing and updating data apply: identify the data you want to access, use the Equals Operator (=), and set the new data to another value, but usually the SAME data type you've originally set. So change data defined as Strings to other Strings, Integers to Integers, and so on.

For example, let's take a look at Jamie and New York from the past chapter:

```
//  NewYork is a CITY
// NewYork has:
// - a name: "New York"
// - a Latitude and Longitude: 40.7127 and 74.0059
// - a Population count: 8406000
City NewYork = new City;
NewYork-NAME = "New York";
NewYork-LATITUDE = 40.7127;
NewYork-LONGITUDE = 74.0059;
NewYork-POPULATION = 8406000;

// Jamie Denise is a person
// She has:
// - a name: Jamie Denise
// - an age: 19
// - a City she lives in: New York
Person Jamie = new Person;
Jamie-NAME = "Jamie Denise";
Jamie-AGE = 19;
Jamie-LOCATION= NewYork
```

So let's say 10 years have passed since we defined Jamie's data object onto our program. Since then, Jamie got married and changed her last name. She also moved to Los Angeles. So how would her new Data Object look like?

You're essentially setting up all your changed data values to their new values. If you wanted to know what these values are, they would give you their current values.

```
// Jamie Walker is a person
// She has:
// - a name: Jamie Walker (changed from Jamie Denise)
// - an age: 29 (was 19)
// - a City she lives in: LosAngeles (was NewYork)
Jamie-NAME = "Jamie Walker";
Jamie-AGE = 29;
Jamie-LOCATION= LosAngeles;
```

and yes, make sure even LosAngeles is defined.

```
//  LosAngeles is a CITY
// LosAngeles has:
// - a name: "Los Angeles"
// - a Latitude and Longitude: 34.0500 and 118.2500
// - a Population count: 3884000
City LosAngeles = new City;
LosAngeles-NAME = "New York";
LosAngeles-LATITUDE = 34.0500;
LosAngeles-LONGITUDE = 118.2500;
LosAngeles-POPULATION = 3884000;
```

## Keeping Track of your Defined Data

let's recall the Clock from the previous chapter:

*Integer HOUR = 20;*
*Integer MINUTE = 30;*

At the moment, it's definitely not 8:30 PM anymore;
let's say it's 10 AM now.

How would the clock change? Easy:

*HOUR = 10;*
*MINUTE = 0;*


Then three and a half hours pass. How would the
clock change? Again, easy.

*HOUR = 13;*
*MINUTE = 30;*

If you wanted the time afterwards, what would it be?
Not 8:30 PM, not 10 AM either. But 1:30 PM.

Here, you've been essentially setting up both your
integers named HOUR and MINUTE to new values.
If you wanted to know what these values are, they
would give you their current values.

However, i**t's Important that you keep track of
your changes. You MUST understand what**

**the changes to your data have been - and you MUST determine whether or not those changes are what you want.**

We stress this because one of the many traits a programmer needs to have (and be good at) is managing what happens to your data.

If you don't believe us, wait until you have your tech interviews for a programming position you're applying for...

# SWIFT-03: Data Changes & Mutable State

### Unchangeable Data Types in Swift

If you declare either atomic data or a Struct as a 'let' definition, you cannot change the data within it.

For example, let's take a look at these two lines:

*let name = "Mandy"*
*name = "Mindy"     // this reports an error*

But of course, Swift wouldn't be a great programming language if the data were so rigid...

So enter Variables

### Variables in Swift

To have changeable data definitions in Swift, use the 'var' variable.

You would define data just as you did before, but you would use 'var' instead of 'let'.

For example, let's revisit the two lines above:

```
var name = "Mandy"
name = "Mindy"     // this WON'T report an error
```

## Changing your Variables' Data Types in Swift

You can't. Once you've set your variable's data type, DO NOT assign a different data type to it. Otherwise, you'll get an error when you try to compile or run your code.

For example, let's revisit the two lines above:

```
// this reports an error: you can't put an Integer
// where a String is supposed to be
var name = "Mandy"
name = 12
```

## Changing Data in Swift

Just like our pseudocode, you can set and reset your Global and Class Variables using the Equals (=) sign.

## Keeping Track of your Data

It's important. Very important. You'll see why in this example...

# SWIFT Workshop #2

### Mountain of Student Debt

(get your IDE ready...)

Let's say you're going back to college to study Computer Science. You've been approved by the bank for a loan for $3000. The Student Loan Balance cannot go over the Loan Limit.

```
// ———
// A Student Loan is an Integer
var studentLoan = 0

// A Loan Limit is an Integer
let loanLimit = 3000

// ———
```

And you also have an online business. You use this to help pay off your loans.

But, knowing the fun-loving person you are, you now have some access to funds for some fun activities...

```
// ———
```

```
// add this code just below the above part:

// Student tuition: 1st Term:
studentLoan += 2500
// Books:
studentLoan += 300
// Paying Off Loan:
studentLoan -= 1000
// Spring Break Trip!
studentLoan += 200
// Unexpected Car Costs:
studentLoan += 600
// Paying Off Loan:
studentLoan -= 1000
// Wild Night Out at the Clubs
studentLoan += 200
// Unexpected Car Costs:
studentLoan += 600
// Paying Off Loan:
studentLoan -= 1000
// Birthday Weekend Trip
studentLoan += 200
// Unexpected Car Costs:
studentLoan += 600
// Paying Off Loan (shorter than usual):
studentLoan -= 200
// Student tuition: 2nd Term:
studentLoan += 1500
// Books:
```

*studentLoan += 300*

*// ———*

Question is, has your balance ever gone above the Student Loan Limit? In real life, of course, that's not supposed to happen at all.

You will have to modify the code to Print out the current Student Loan balance after

If you're a bit more advanced, you can add more sophisticated code if you wish.

The key learning experience here is for you to understand how crucial it is to keep track of your data. There are many aspects of coding that depend on it, such as Debugging and making sure your code works the way you intend it to.

# Chapter 5a: Defining & Designing your Functions

Now we'll move on to the parts of programming where the magic happens.

Functions.

Where data structures are used to represent "things" in this universe, you define functions as the "actions" or verbs in this universe.

And you can make your functions do whatever you want/need it to do, as long as you know what you're doing. You can calculate math, write sentences for you, change or update data, sort out lists with tens of thousands of items, make websites for you, whatever you like. In reality, the possibilities can be endless.

But first let's understand the core parts of function design: its inputs, its output, its signature, its effects, and its functionality.

### A Function's Inputs

You can set your function to accept whatever data you need it to.

These are called a function's arguments or parameters. Your function will use this incoming data to perform what you intend it to.

Or, on the other hand, you can also have a function NOT require any inputs. Your function will then perform what you've programmed it to, but it won't need any incoming data.

For practice, let's use comments to declare what inputs we want our function to have. Let's say we want a name (a string) as an input

*// INPUT: - a name (String)*

**A Function's Output**

Your function can also return a data value - based on whatever you want to set it to. You can then program your function to output that same data type.

Or, you can also have a function NOT return anything. You can then program your function to do what you intend it to do, but it won't return any data after it executes.

In most programming languages, functions only return ONE thing - whether it be a data value, an entire list, compound data, or more.

However, you must make sure your function outputs whatever you have set it to. Say, if you want your function to output a String, the very last line of that function MUST return a String data type. If you set your function to have no outputs, your function MUST NOT return any data types after it executes.

For practice, let's use comments to declare what outputs we want our function to have. We'll continue designing our function. We now have an input, now we want to have an output.

*// INPUT: - a name (String)*
*// OUTPUT: - an ID (Number)*


## Defining what your Function will Do

Now we figure out what EFFECT our function will have once we run it.

This is your function's main purpose - it's the reason why you're going to write these lines of code!

Your function's effect will be whatever you intend it to do. Change data, create new data, calculate a few values together, whatever you want.

But isn't an Output and Effect the same thing? Well, no.

There is a difference between a function's OUTPUT and EFFECT. A function's output is the data it returns, while a function's effect is anything that the function does or anything the function's action has affected.

For practice, let's use comments to declare what effects we want our function to have. We'll continue designing our function. We now have an input and output. Now we figure out what it does when we run it.

Let's say we want it to come up with a random number. We first put in the comments of what we intend it to do

*// INPUT: - a name (String)*
*// OUTPUT: - an ID (Number)*
*// EFFECT: generates a random number for a given name*

## Key Function Rule-of-Thumb:

Make sure your function only does the only one thing you want it to do. A function that does too many things will not only complicate your code and make it look bad, but it will cause headaches and frustration for programming teammates.

However, your function can include and call on many other functions to help process something. These are called Helper Functions (we'll cover this later!)

## A Function's Signature

Here is when we start writing our function's lines of code.

In most programming languages, a function's signature defines a function's name, inputs, outputs, and even particular traits it has.

Remember when we declared our Composite data? We first started out designing the name of our whole data structure, then we started designing what it consisted of.

For function signatures, we first code what its name is - as well as any inputs and outputs it has.

Now, let's look back at the function we were designing for practice. We now know what it does, what it requires and what it returns.

For now, we'll use Pseudocode to design our function's Signature. Our signatures will then be structured in this form:

(OutputType) functionName(InputType inputName)

So our function's signature will look like this:

*// INPUT: - a name (String)*
*// OUTPUT: - an ID (Number)*

*// EFFECT: generates a random number for a given name*
*name*
*number createID(string name)*

## Implementing your Function

This can be the tricky part - unless you know exactly what you're doing.

In designing functions, the last thing you do is to program your function's actual functionality. You would now know what inputs & outputs it has, as well as what it's trying to do. You've essentially planned what your function will do.

Now you'll have your function do what you planned it to.

You program the functionality in the next few lines after your function's signature.

In pseudocode, we'll use curly brackets ( { } ) right after the function's signature to include its functionality code. Our functions will then be structured in this form:

(OutputType) functionName(InputType inputName)
{

    (your function's code)

    return OutputType if any

}

Finally, let's look back at the function we were designing for practice. We are ready to finish it.

Let's say there's such thing as a function named randomNumber() that creates a random number for us.

```
// INPUT: - a name (String)
// OUTPUT: - an ID (Number)
// EFFECT: generates a random number for a given
name
number createID(string name) {
        randomNumber()
}
```

## A Common Error in Function Design

But wait. The above code isn't going to work. Can you guess why?

Oh right.

In our signature, our function is supposed to RETURN a number. So in order for this function to work, it needs to actually return a number.

So we make the function RETURN whatever random number is generated by the inside function randomNumber()

```
// INPUT: - a name (String)
// OUTPUT: - an ID (Number)
// EFFECT: generates a random number for a given
name
number createID(string name) {
        return randomNumber()
}
```

and now, we finally complete our function - from design to code.

### Calling your Function Procedure

To have your code execute whatever effect or procedure you've defined in your functions, you simply put your function name in your code - but in a particular way

Keep in mind that you can only place your function wherever its output data type is expected to be. The exception is when your function has no data output (returns void). You can place this function on lines by itself.

For example, take these two functions:

```
// INPUT: - none
// OUTPUT: - an ID (Number)
// EFFECT: ?????
number procedureA() {...}
```

```
// INPUT: - none
// OUTPUT: - none
// EFFECT: ?????
void procedureB() {...}
```

Procedure A outputs a number. Place the function wherever the data type Number is expected:

```
Number x = procedureA();
Number y = 10.213 * procedureA();
```

Procedure A outputs nothing. Place the function on its own line of code.

```
procedureB();
```

If a function belongs to a data class, make sure to access that function from an instance of that data class:

*ClassC instanceC = new ClassC;*
*instanceC.procedureC();*

# Chapter 5b: Matching Data with Functions

Here's an inevitable truth when it comes to functions: they will almost always involve data in any way.

Later on, you'll find that all sorts of different data structures will have at least one key function associated with it.

Also, some data structures, by default, will have associated go-to templates to use in programming. Remember this well; if you're given a certain data structure to work with, you should already have the function structure you'll need in mind.

## Functions using Atomic Data

There's usually no structure or template involved when dealing with Atomic Data.

Functions may have atomic data as inputs or outputs when necessary.

Here are some pseudocode to demonstrate:

// INPUT: - a Name (String)
// OUTPUT: - an ID (Number)
// EFFECT: ?????
number procedureA(String name) {... return ID}

// INPUT: - none
// OUTPUT: - none
// EFFECT: ?????
void procedureB() {...}


Also, Functions can even modify existing variables.

// Player1 Score, as an Integer
Integer Score = 0

// INPUT: - none
// OUTPUT: - none
// EFFECT: increments the score by one
void score1() { Score += 1}

## Functions using Composite Data

The key thing to remember here is that, for every component a composite data structure has, its associated function will have a template that accesses and deals with each component (regardless of what data type each component is). Also, each component will be treated as whatever data type it is; a String treated as a String, composite data as composite data, and so on.

We demonstrate this in pseudocode:

```
// Structure of a Book:
CompositeStructure Book {
        String AUTHOR
        String TITLE
        Integer PAGECOUNT
}

// INPUT: - a Book
// OUTPUT: - none
// EFFECT: ?????
void bookTemplateFunc(Book b) {
        b.AUTHOR //do something
        b.TITLE // do something
        b.PAGECOUNT // do something
}
```

Here's an example of a printing function, based on the above template:

```
// INPUT: - a Book
// OUTPUT: - none
// EFFECT: prints book details
void printDetails(Book b) {
        printString(b.AUTHOR)
        printString(b.TITLE)
        printInteger(b.PAGECOUNT )
```

*}*

## Methods: Functions for Object-Oriented Programming

In Object-oriented programming, data and procedures are bundled in data structures called classes.

Functions are called Methods and class variables are called Fields.

You can think of Methods within a class as 'behaviours' - or what actions an instance of that class can do.

To describe Class Methods in comments, simply list the behaviours it can do:

*// A Space Invaders Tank Class can:*
*// - move left*
*// - move right*
*// - shoot a missile*

*// A Dog Class can:*
*// - walk*

*// - bark*
*// - sit*
*// - eat*

## Functions for Sequences

(You'll cover this in later chapters...)

Basically, data elements of the same type can be grouped together into sequenced collections. Examples can be lists and strings.

For these, functions process each element one by one until all data elements are covered.

## Functions for more Sophisticated Data Structures

(You'll cover this in later chapters...)

# SWIFT-04: Function Structure

### Functions in Swift

You're very fortunate to learn functions the way the book has described.

Because, similar to Java, C, and C++, Swift functions require what data types will be inputs and outputs. You will have to define your data inputs and outputs in your Swift Function code.

Overall, the syntax structure for Swift functions are so:

```
func functionName(<inputName>: <input DataType>)-><output DataType> {

        // (your function's actions here)

        return (data must match output DataType)

}
```

As a VERY important note, our pseudocode is a close representation of all other languages. Within the function parameters, the parameter name follows the data type. However, in Swift, this is reversed: the data type follows the parameter name.

There are a few key notes in Swift Functions:

- Swift functions always start with the word 'func', then your function name, then parentheses along with any inputs, then curly brackets along with any code you have.

- In Swift, if your functions have inputs (aka arguments or parameters), you will have to declare them within the parentheses after your function name. For example, if your function has a String data type as an input, your parentheses would look like so: (inputName: String)

- If you have multiple inputs, just use a comma to separate them. For example: (input1: String, input2: Number)

- Function outputs in Swift need to be declared. If your function has an output, you must have a line within your function body (between the curly braces) that returns the data type you've declared. So if your function returns a String, you must have a line that says 'return "(whatever string)" ' or 'return x', where x is set to a String.

- If your Swift function has no data outputs, simply set its output type to 'Void'.

## Atomic Data Type Names in Swift

In Swift, since you have to declare the various atomic data types in your Function Definitions, it's important to know the proper syntax for each type:

for Strings: String

for Integers: Int

for Booleans: Bool

for floats: Float

## Function Example

Here's what the createID() function looks like in Swift:

*// INPUT: - a name (String)*

```
// OUTPUT: - an ID (Number)
// EFFECT: generates a random number for a given
name
func createID(name: String)->Number {
        return randomNumber()
}
```

# SWIFT Workshop #3

## Designing & Calling Functions

First, go to an IDE of your choice. An online IDE such as SwiftStub (swiftstub.com), or even the Xcode app will do.

Then, copy-paste the code between the dotted lines:

```
// - - - - - - - - - - - - - - - - - - - - - - - - - - -
class calculator{

        // INPUT: - two Integers
        // OUTPUT: - a result(Integer)
         // EFFECT: add two integers together & give
result
        func add(a: ___, b:___)->___{
        return a + b;
        }

        // INPUT: - two Integers
        // OUTPUT: - a result(Integer)
         // EFFECT: subtract 1st integer from 2nd &
give result
        func subtract(a: ___, b:___)->___{
        return ____;
        }
```

```
    }

// INPUT: - a String
// OUTPUT: - nothing (Void)
// EFFECT: prints the string input
func printer(s:____)->____ {
  println(s)
}

// Your Bank Account is an Integer
var BANKACCOUNT = 0

// Create a Calculator Object
let c = calculator()

// Income & Expenses, as Integers
let PAYCHEQUE = 7000
let LIVINGEXP = 4000
let FUNSTUFF = 2000
let TRAVEL = 4000


// How much would fun stuff and travel be
together?
let FUNTRAVEL = c.add(___, b:___)
printer("Fun Stuff & Travel Together: " +
String(FUNTRAVEL))
```

*// Your Paycheque, minus paying your living expenses?*

*// (HINT: call the calculator object c, then access one of its methods. . .)*

*BANKACCOUNT = c.____(____, b:____)*

*printer("Bank Account Balance, normal:" + String(BANKACCOUNT))*

*// Your Paycheque, after paying your living expenses AND fun stuff?*

*// (HINT: call the calculator object c, then access one of its methods. . .)*

*// (HINT: the printer() returns Void, aka nothing. Use it on a line on its own!)*

*BANKACCOUNT = _____*

*BANKACCOUNT = _____*

*____("Bank Account Balance, w/ Fun Stuff: " + String(BANKACCOUNT))*

*// - - - - - - - - - - - - - - - - - - - - - - - - -*

Before you begin, your code should look exactly to the code above.

Now, fill in the blanks.

If you filled in the blanks with proper code, you should have the printed lines below:

*Fun Stuff & Travel Together: 6000*
*Bank Account Balance, normal: 3000*
*Bank Account Balance, w/ Fun Stuff: 1000*

Good luck!

# Chapter 6: Intro to Designing Worlds & Simple Apps, PT1

At this point, you know how to interpret real-life objects as computer data representations, as well as interpreting actions & procedures as programming functions.

Now, you'll begin the design process. You start to describe virtual worlds and apps, almost always visually. You prepare to translate your ideas into code and data.

Just as if you were a carpenter thinking of how to build your house, you use the same approach towards developing apps and game worlds. You identify all the components required to build your project.

### Simple App Design Process

There are three key things about your idea that you need to identify: the facts behind your idea, what remains constant, and what will change/vary.

The reason for this is to give you and other programmers as much control and stability over your data as possible. You would know what type of data you would be working with and if/how that data would or would not change. Experienced programmers can then check if a particular data structure or function is designed the way it was intended to be.

To guide you through this process, we'll describe the classic Snake game - and identify plenty of details about the game from a programmer's standpoint. It will be as if we're designing the game for the first time. As if we're in the 70's.

**Identifying the FACTS**

First, you need the facts. You need to describe what your idea is about, what's involved, etc. Describe as much detail as you can, including the environment and key figures you provide.

Example:

In a single game of Snake, there exists a snake with a head and body, as well as food items that appear randomly. The snake's head, all segments of its body, and the food pieces have an X-Y coordinate and a visual representation (since they have similar traits, they can be grouped together as a game sprite). An X-Y coordinate represents a location within the playable zone: a rectangular area with a height and width. A score keeps track of how many food items have been eaten.

The player changes which direction the snake will travel to: up, down, left, and right. The game ends when the snake either hits a wall or runs into one of its body segments.

The snake grows by one body segment after the snake head "eats a food item" (appears on the same coordinate as a food item).

[food] + [head] [body] [body]

=

[head] [body] [body] [body]

## Identifying what's CONSTANT

Second, you need to identify what elements in your world or app remain consistent throughout the programming. Also, identify what will exist in your idea unconditionally.

Example:

The food items, snake head, and body segments have consistent images.

The playing board has a fixed width and height.

## Identifying what CHANGES/VARIES

Third, identify what will change or vary when the program runs.

Example:

The food items, snake head, and body segments all have varying X-Y coordinates throughout the game. The number of body segments vary, from the initial number of 2, all the way to as much as possible.

## Turning your ideas into code

Now, you take note of all the facts, descriptions, and ideas you've come up with. You'll be making data representations of them.

Early in the book, there is a great reason why we've used comments to describe all the information we are going to create. It's because they help select the best possible data representation for each pint of information you have. And after you've described what your app or world will be about, you'll start developing that digital world first by using comments.

Example:

For each fact and idea about the Snake game that we've come up with, we'll use comments to hint how they should be represented by data.

*// A Game Sprite has:*
*// - an X-coordinate (Integer)*
*// - a Y-coordinate (Integer)*
*// - an image to represent itself (choose your visual representation)*

*// Snake Heads, Snake Body Segments, and Food Pieces*

```
// are each represented by Game Sprites

// An EntireSnake contains:
// - a Snake Head (GameSprite)
// - a list of Snake Body Segments (list of
GameSprites)
// A FullSnake can:
// - eat food
// - grow
// - move on the board

// The Playable Board has:
// - a fixed length (Integer)
// - a fixed width (Integer)

// A Game of Snake has:
// - a playable board (Playable Board Class)
// - food items (list of Food)
// - the Snake (EntireSnake)
// - a Score Count (Integer)
// A Game of Snake can:
// - start a new game
// - end the game (as a loss or win)
// - update a game in progress
// - update the score
// - move the snake on keypresses
// - create or delete food items
```

Notice how there is no actual code written yet; only comments. The beauty of this process is that, given the facts and ideas (as well as their data representations), we can start creating the code in any language we want. We now know what will be data structures, classes, integers, and so on.

We do need to go over more tools, so we will continue with design later on.

Meanwhile, in the next big workshop, you will be converting idea comments into actual code. Good luck and have fun!

# SWIFT BIG Workshop A

## Game Design: the Data & Functions

First, go to an IDE of your choice, such as SwiftStub (swiftstub.com), or the Xcode app.

You're going to practice designing Data Structures and Functions - as if you were designing an app yourself.

All you'll be given is a set of comments describing the data objects within a very, very simple video game. If you can, you may continue developing it into a full-blown game.

Copy and paste all the comment code below, then start writing code for the data definitions.

As you improve your programming and learn more tricks over time, you can revisit this workshop and re-create it using your new skills.

For example: for the functions and class methods, they might need more intermediate functionality. So you can come back to them later - after going through the necessary chapters.

If you feel like you want to create or remove new Fields, Classes, or Methods, feel free to do so.

Now, let's move forward.

The game we'll be designing is...

PONG!

Good luck!

// - - - - - -   - - - - -   - - - - -   - - - - -   - - - - -

*// A Game Sprite Class has:*
*// - a Width (Integer)*
*// - a Height (Integer)*
*// - an X-coordinate (Integer)*
*// - a Y-coordinate (Integer)*


*// A Ball Class has:*
*// - all properties of a Game Sprite*
*// - either an UP or DOWN direction (String)*
*// - either a LEFT or RIGHT direction (String)*
*// A Ball Class can:*
*// - move in all 4 diagonal directions*

```
// - bounce off Paddles or the Game Board Up/
Down Walls

// A Paddle Class has:
// - all properties of a Game Sprite
// A Paddle Class can:
// - move up & move down

// A Player Class has:
// - a Paddle
// - a Score (Integer)
// A Player Class Can:
// - Score a Goal

// a Game Board has:
// - a Width (Integer)
// - a Height (Integer)
// - two X-Coordinates for Player-side Edges
(Integers, set to 0 and Width)
// - two Y-Coordinates for Up-Down Walls
(Integers, set to 0 and Height)

// A Game Class has:
// - two Paddles
// - a Ball
// - a Game Board
// - a Player on the Left
// - a Player on the Right
// - a Game Speed (Strings: "SLOW" "MEDIUM", or
"FAST")
```

// - a Timer (a Number, Integer, or any other Data Type you like)
// When Created, A Game Instance also creates:
// - a Paddle for the Left Player
// - a Left Player
// - a Right Player
// - a Paddle for the Right Player
// - a Ball, moving at a given random direction
// A Game Class can:
// - manage a goal scored by either player
// - end the game
// - declare a winning player


// - - - - - -  - - - - -  - - - - -  - - - - -  - - - - -

# PART II: Special Function & Method Tools

# Chapter 7: IF & ELSE statements

Among all programming languages, the concept of IF & Else statements is quite simple: a few lines of code will either execute or not, depending on certain conditions.

## Importance

IF/ELSE statements will be one of the most frequently used code in programming. As a matter of fact. more advanced code will depend on these statements often.

## Analysis

In pseudocode, here is a sample IF-ELSE statement:

```
// EFFECT: check condition A
// - run True Procedure on TRUE
// - run False Procedure on FALSE
if (conditionA == TRUE) {
      // EXECUTABLE CODE:
      trueProcedure();
}
else {
      // ELSE-STATEMENT CODE
      falseProcedure();
```

*}*

Now, let's analyze the parts of the code above.

**Signature**

As always, it's best practice to describe your code's functionality before creating it.

If you recall Programming Functions from a previous chapter, functions have a certain effect you intend it to perform once it has been called. IF/ELSE statements are also meant to create an effect (given the condition holds true) wherever you place them in your code.

In our signature, we describe our IF/ELSE statement with the conditions we look for and the effects we want to occur.

```
// EFFECT: check condition A
// - run True Procedure on TRUE
// - run False Procedure on FALSE
```

**Parts of the IF statement**

In almost all programming languages, there are three parts to an IF statement. The first is the word 'if'; here, your code declares an IF statement. The second and third are the Condition and the Executable Code.

*if (....) {*
*.....*
*};*

## Condition

In an If Statement, we place our pseudocode within parentheses "( )" as the condition. The   code in the condition must return a boolean - either TRUE or FALSE. Here, you can use fields that contain booleans, compare two values using operators ( ==, ! =, >, <, and more), or even use boolean operators (AND, NOT, OR)

*if (conditionA == TRUE) {*
*.....*
*};*

## Executable Code

After the condition returns true, the program will execute all code after it - all the way until the end of the code line.

But if the condition returns false, the program will skip the executable code and move on.

In Pseudocode, for multiple lines of executable code, we place them within curly brackets "{ }".

```
if (conditionA == TRUE) runFunctionA();
if (conditionB == TRUE) {
    runFunctionB();
    runFunctionC();
};
```

## ELSE Statement

After the condition returns false, the program will skip over the Executable Code. But if you have an ELSE statement, the program will instead execute all code following that ELSE statement - all the way until the end of the code line. In pseudocode, multiple lines of executable code are also placed within curly brackets "{ }".

```
if (conditionA == TRUE) runFunctionA();
else {
```

```
        runFunctionB();
        runFunctionC();
};
```

# Chapter 8: Helper Functions

The concept behind helper functions is quite simple.

A larger, complex, general function will call other smaller, more specialized functions to achieve its given purpose.

And to do this, you must remember one important thing...

**A Key Concept: The Small Parts of the Whole**

If it's one thing you need to learn about programming that encompasses EVERY single aspect of programming, it's this one phrase:

*"Break down a large concept into several smaller parts, then again into even smaller parts, until you have the very basic elements. Define and create what each of those basic elements are, then continue building your concept until it's finished."*

For example, if you've read up to the chapter where you've designed the Snake Game, you've noticed that creating an app follows the above: break down the large app into several data structures, which then are further broken down into either other Data Structures or atomic data types.

In this chapter, we'll apply this large-to-small concept towards Functions and Class Methods.

And the best way to explore the Helper Function concept is to see it in action.

**Example: Robotic Legs**

Take a look at this method for the class Droid, in Pseudocode. Assume that it's part of a larger, working, artificial intelligence program for the Droid:

```
// INPUT: - none
// OUTPUT: - none
// EFFECT: Droid walks forward across terrain,
using its feet, unless there is something the droid
cannot walk over.
void walk() {
        // check for obstacles in the front
        // return if droid cannot walk over obstacle
        if (frontSensor.detectsObject
```

*& objectDetected.height >*
*Droid.height / 2*
       *& objectDetected.distance <= 1Foot)*
*return*

      *// check if left foot is currently behind right foot*
*// make a left foot step if so*
*if (rightFoot.y > leftFoot.y) {*
*rightFoot.transferBalance()*
*leftLeg.lift()*
*rightFoot.moveBalanceForward()*
*leftFoot.moveForward(PastOtherFoot)*
*leftFoot.placeOnGround()*

      *// check if right foot is currently behind left foot*
*// make a right foot step if so*
*if (leftFoot.y > rightFoot.y) {*
*leftFoot.transferBalance()*
*right Leg.lift()*
*leftFoot.moveBalanceForward()*
*rightFoot.moveForward(PastOtherFoot)*
*rightFoot.placeOnGround()*
*}*

Since this code works correctly, there really are no coding errors with this code.

However, the class method walk() is far too long and not quite pleasant to look at. And also, for a single method, it does far too many things. If a single error were to occur on this code, the debugging process would be extremely difficult. The programmer would have to review every single phrase of code to figure out what's wrong.

(But hey, At least the walk() method already uses helper functions on plenty of its lines. The code could be worse. Instead of the code above, what if a majority of the lines within the walk() method moved every single droid-muscle required, in every angle necessary, and moved every single leg part to the space it's supposed to be in? That would be a lot of lines...)

Remember when we mentioned "breaking down large concepts into smaller parts?" Let's do it for the walk() method. We're going to see how many related lines of code can we condense into smaller methods.

**The Helper Functions**

The first helper function we can make is this IF statement:

> *if (frontSensor.detectsObject*
> *&  o b j e c t D e t e c t e d . h e i g h t  >*
> *Droid.height / 2*
> *& objectDetected.distance <= 1Foot)*

That is quite a handful for just a conditional portion.

What if we can simplify it into a Helper Function? We know that the entire conditional takes no inputs and outputs a boolean.

```
// INPUT: - none
// OUTPUT: - boolean
// EFFECT: returns TRUE if Droid detects an
obstacle it cannot walk over
boolean checkObstacle() {
        frontSensor.detectsObject
        & objectDetected.height > Droid.height / 2
        & objectDetected.distance <= 1Foot
}
```

Then, the IF-statement turns into just this:

*if (checkObstacle()) return*

Next, remember the two stepping portions? They were quite lengthy, weren't they?

But what if we turned them both into Helper Functions? They would have distinct, focused functionality. Also, they would look cleaner and more simple. Here, we will name them leftFootStep() and rightFootStep(), respectively:

```
// INPUT: - none
// OUTPUT: - none
// EFFECT: make a left foot step if left foot is
currently behind right foot
void leftFootStep() {
        if (rightFoot.y > leftFoot.y) {
        rightFoot.transferBalance()
        leftLeg.lift()
        rightFoot.moveBalanceForward()
        leftFoot.moveForward(PastOtherFoot)
        leftFoot.placeOnGround()
        }
}

// INPUT: - none
// OUTPUT: - none
// EFFECT: make a right foot step if right foot is
currently behind left foot
void rightFootStep() {
        if (leftFoot.y > rightFoot.y) {
        leftFoot.transferBalance()
        right Leg.lift()
        leftFoot.moveBalanceForward()
        rightFoot.moveForward(PastOtherFoot)
        rightFoot.placeOnGround()
        }
}
```

## The Larger Function

After converting significant portions of code into helper functions, the walk() method now calls each helper function where necessary. All functions now have a single purpose

```
// INPUT: - none
// OUTPUT: - none
// EFFECT: Droid walks forward across terrain
void walk() {
        if (checkObstacle()) return
        leftFootStep()
        rightFootStep()
}
```

Do you notice how much cleaner and simple the method walk() is now?

And if you had to debug something, it would be much more simple. If there's an error in the programming about checking obstacles or stepping with either foot, you can focus on that specific helper function and any code inside it.

## Putting it All Together

The concept behind helper functions is simple: for a bigger, general function, give it a general purpose, then have it call other smaller single-purpose functions to help achieve its purpose.

This applies to all programming languages as well.

# Chapter 9: Local Variables

## The Function, and Its Locals

You can define variables within a function/method to hold key data for that function/method to use.

These are called Local Variables, or locals for short.

Later on, you will need locals for more advanced concepts, such as accumulator variables and even within algorithms.

## Local Variables V.S. Global Variables

Here are the key differences between Local and Global variables.

Global variables can be accessed and will exist throughout your entire code file.

Local Variables can only be accessed within the functions/methods they're defined in. They'll also be gone once your function finishes running.

## Defining Locals

In most programming languages, you would simply define a local variable as if you were defining a global one. The difference is that you define the local variable within the function code only.

Here is a pseudocode example where we define local variables, as opposed to global variables:

```
String GLOBAL1 = "aaa"
Integer GLOBAL2 = 123
Boolean GLOBAL3 = TRUE

// INPUT: - none
// OUTPUT: - none
// EFFECT: ?????
void functionName() {
        String LOCAL1 = "aaa"
        Integer LOCAL2 = 123
        Boolean LOCAL3 = TRUE
}
```

## Referencing a Local Variable Properly

These next few rules may vary depending on the programming language you're working with, but these generally apply to most of them (if not all).

Here are some key rules in accessing Global v.s. Local Variables:

1) Local variables can only be accessed within the same function code.

2) Global variables can be accessed throughout the code file - whether or not it's accessed inside a function.

3) Depending on which programming language, local variable names may or may not have the exact name as an existing global variable. If the language allows it, you might need to distinctly identify which variable you are accessing.

Now let's take a look at these lines of pseudocode:

```
String GLOBAL1 = "aaa"
Integer GLOBAL2 = 123
Boolean GLOBAL3 = TRUE
String SAMEVAR = "samevar"
(any type) ACCESS3 = _____

// INPUT: - none
// OUTPUT: - none
// EFFECT: ?????
void function1() {
        String LOCAL1 = "aaa"
        Integer LOCAL2 = 123
        Boolean LOCAL3 = TRUE
        String SAMEVAR = "samevar"
```

        *(any type) ACCESS1 = _____*
}

*// INPUT: - none*
*// OUTPUT: - none*
*// EFFECT: ?????*
*void function2() {*
        *String LOCAL4 = "aaa"*
        *Integer LOCAL5 = 123*
        *Boolean LOCAL6 = TRUE*
        *String SAMEVAR = "samevar"*
        *(any type) ACCESS2 = _____*
}

The code within function1() cannot access the locals within function2(), and vice versa. Hence, ACCESS1 and ACCESS2 cannot refer to any locals, respectively, within function2() and function1().

Both functions can access the Global Variables. Hence, ACCESS1 and ACCESS2 can refer to any global variable.

However, any code outside the functions cannot access its locals. Hence, ACCESS3 cannot refer to any locals within function2() and function1().

The rules within each programming language will differ about the third rule. If somehow our pseudocode allows local/global variables with same names, you'll need to identify which variable you're referring to. For example, if ACCESS1 and ACCESS2 were to refer to SAMEVAR, they can refer to either the locals within their respective functions, or refer to the global SAMEVAR:

*// refer to Local*
*(any type) ACCESS1 = SAMEVAR*

*// or refer to Global*
*(any type) ACCESS1 = global SAMEVAR*

## Putting it All Together

Despite a few rules about local variables, you'll find how important they'll be in the chapters to come. Functions with the ability to store data themselves will open many programming possibilities.

# PART III: Operators and Logic

# Chapter 10: Boolean Logic and Operators

For every line or expression that needs to return a Boolean, use these operators to compare values together.

It's best to compare Atomic Data Types, such as Strings, Integers, Numbers and even Booleans themselves. Remember: Some programming languages are more strict about what data types you use as values; and some are more lax.

You can also compare Function and Method outputs, as we'll show later, but you have to make sure that they return the exact data types that you'll be comparing.

Boolean Logic is particularly important for managing more sophisticated algorithms, functions, and methods - so take note.

**Basic Boolean Logic:**

The three basic Boolean Operators are AND, OR, and NOT. Use these to compare booleans together.

Speaking of comparing booleans, if you compare booleans together using the boolean operators from above, you'll get a result based on the below:

## The AND operator:

Using the AND operator, comparing two values together will return TRUE - if, and only if, both values are true.

TRUE and TRUE returns TRUE

TRUE and FALSE returns FALSE

FALSE and TRUE returns FALSE

FALSE and FALSE returns FALSE


## The OR operator:

Comparing two values together using the OR operator will return TRUE - if at least one value is true.

TRUE or TRUE returns TRUE

TRUE or FALSE returns TRUE

FALSE or TRUE returns TRUE

FALSE or FALSE returns FALSE

**Multiple Boolean Operators:**

You can also compare multiple boolean values together. But to keep things simple (and not mess up your code), make sure you're only comparing with either the AND or OR operator - but not both.

(TRUE and FALSE and FALSE and TRUE) returns FALSE

(TRUE or FALSE or TRUE or FALSE) returns TRUE

**The NOT operator:**

You can convert a single Boolean into its opposite value using the NOT operator.

not TRUE returns FALSE

not FALSE returns TRUE

## Function Outputs and Variables

You can compare these values using Boolean Operators with Functions that return a Boolean as a data type.

Here's an example in Pseudocode:

```
// INPUT: - two integers
// OUTPUT: - Boolean
// EFFECT: check if 1st integer is larger than 2nd one
Boolean check(Integer a, Integer b) {
        return a > b
}
```

```
// will print TRUE
print(check(12, 1) and check(100, 1))
```

You can also compare variables that hold booleans. In most languages, they can be any variable type.

Here's an example in Pseudocode:

```
// Two Global Variables that hold Booleans
Boolean YOUARECOOL = true
Boolean YOUAREAWESOME = true
```

```
// will print TRUE
print(YOUARECOOL or YOUAREAWESOME)
```

# Chapter 11: Fundamental Programming Operators

These operators are designed to either manipulate your data or compare/contrast two values together.

These operators are frequently used to develop functionality - from complex algorithms to simple functions. Programmers will almost always use these operators well.

An important note here is to use these operators with a purpose. The point behind leaving comments to describe your code does just that. If you - or your colleague - were trying to compare two values together, you would use comments to describe what's required. Afterwards, whoever is writing the actual code can add the right functionality to your code.

Again, it's best to compare Atomic Data Types, such as Strings, Integers, Numbers and even Booleans themselves.

Just like the Boolean Operators, you can compare Function and Method outputs, but you have to make sure that they return the exact data types that you'll be comparing.

**Comparison operators:**

These are what you use to compare a value greater than/ less than /or equal to another value.

In most languages, you can use these to compare Integers and Numbers. So either variables with those data types or functions/methods that return those types.

Greater Than: (your data) > _____

Greater Than or Equal to: (your data) >= _____

Less Than: (your data) < _____

Less Than or equal to: (your data) <= _____

**Equality operators:**

Use these operators between to values to compare whether or not two values are equal to each other.

Is Equal To: (value1) == (value2)

Is NOT Equal To: (value1) != (value2)

In most languages, the '==' and '!=' will be consistently compare two values for equality.

## The General Assignment operator:

This is simply using the Equals Sign (=) to assign data.

Yes, you must have been using this the whole time! We just wanted to keep things simple and add steps one at a time.

Just to be sure, it was set up like this:

(1st Variable Name) = (Value or expression to change 1st Variable Value to);

## Mathematic Assignment operators:

These are similar to the general assignment operator (a single equals sign, '='; the same operator you set your variables!). However, in most languages, you can modify the left-hand value using the right-hand-value, depending on what your Assignment Operator is:

(1st Variable Name) (Assignment Operator) (Value to change 1st Variable Value to)

Essentially, there will be an added character before the Equals Sign; this character will determine what value your Assignment Operator is.

In most programming languages, these assignment operators will be consistent throughout:

%= /= //= -= += *= **=     Assignment operators

Add to the 1st Value:       (1st Value) += (Value to Add)

Multiply the 1st Value: (1st Value) *=       (Value to Multiply)

Divide the 1st Value: (1st Value) /=  (Value to Divide)

Modulus to the 1st Value: (1st Value) &= (Value to Divide, without Remainders)

For obvious reasons, these are best used with numerical data types - such as Integers and Numbers. Of course, we need numbers to do math with!

# SWIFT-05: Boolean Operators in SWIFT

**Logic Operators.**

In SWIFT, the Three Basic Logic Operators are so:

AND operator:       &&

OR operator:       ||

NOT operator:       !     (just a single exclamation mark)

Here's a few examples in SWIFT Code:

*// Returns false:*
*println (true && false)*
*// Returns true:*
*println (true || false)*
*// Returns false:*
*println (!true)*

**Comparison operators:**

In SWIFT, the same characters from the pseudocode (>, <, and =) are used as comparison operators.

You can try these out. Run these lines of code:

```
// These print true
println (17 > 15)
println (17 >= 17)
println (12 < 15)
println (12 <= 12)
// These print false
println (0 > 15)
println (11 >= 15)
println (100 < 15)
println (16 <= 15)
```

**Equality operators:**

These operators are also the same characters as the Pseudocode.

Try these out:

```
// Prints true
println ("xyz" == "xyz")
// Prints true
println ("aab" != "aaa")
```

**Mathematic Assignment operators:**

Yep, same as our operators:

```
// 'aa' is a variable set to Integer 3
var aa = 3
// This should print 6 twice
aa = 3
aa += 3
println (aa)
aa = 3
aa *= 2
println (aa)


// This should print 1 three times
aa = 3
aa -= 2
println (aa)
aa = 3
aa /= 3
println (aa)
aa = 3
aa %= 2
println (aa)
```

# SWIFT Workshop #4

## Working with Operators

First, go to an IDE of your choice. Online IDE's include Rextester (rextester.com), CodeChef (www.codechef.com/ide), CodePad (codepad.org), and Ideone (https://ideone.com/).

Copy-paste the lines below (between the dashed lines) into your IDE of choice.

Then, fill in the blanks with whichever operator you wish. Go ahead and have fun with it.

Keep in mind the difference between operators that return Booleans, and operators that change data values!

```
// - - - - - - - - - - - - - - - - - - - - - - - - - - - -

// INPUT: - an age (Integer)
// OUTPUT: - none
// EFFECT: prints some random message per given age
func ageLifeTeller(age:Int)->Void {
    if age < 5 {
```

```
        println( "Just a Baby" ) }
    else if age >= 5 && age <= 17
        { println( "Just a School Kid") }
    else
        { println( "A Fully Responsible Adult!") }

}



var x = 4
ageLifeTeller(x)
x = 16
ageLifeTeller(x)
x ___ 2
ageLifeTeller(x)
x ___ 2
ageLifeTeller(x)
x = 21
ageLifeTeller(x)
x ___ 3
ageLifeTeller(x)
x ___ 3
ageLifeTeller(x)


// - - - - - - - - - - - - -- - - - - - - -- - - - -- - - - -
```

# PART IV: Lists

# Chapter 12a: Lists

At one point, computers will eventually have a collection of data to deal with - regardless whether they are objects or basic data.

Thus, we have lists.

## Lists in General

As an Abstract Data Type, lists are essentially a series of data items connected together.

Computers will generally go through data item on the lists one by one.

There are two general types of lists: linked lists and arrays. Most programming languages will usually include either type of list.

## Linked Lists v.s. Arrays. Which list to use?

IMPORTANT NOTE: The ironic thing about most programming languages is the fact that they ALL have arrays and linked lists available. But, what if a colleague or boss asks you which one to use? See, sometimes making the slightest decisions like these will be such big deals that make or break an app - and sometimes, even job applications, careers and startups.

In general, use Linked Lists for quickly adding and deleting data items for that list, no matter what order they are. Whether the item is first, last, or in the middle of the list, it takes the same time and effort for the computer to add/remove data items. Also, if you also don't know how big your list will be, linked lists are preferable.

In general, use Arrays for any computing where you need to access or process each element in the list. The indices in the Array will help your computer process the list faster, as well as give your computer multi-process potential for that list. Also, use arrays if each item in the list needs an index. For example, if you wanted to randomly get list items, you can only do it in an array (in a linked list, how would the computer know what item to get? Think about it...)

Bottom line:

Linked Lists = any size, faster add/remove

Arrays = fixed size, faster access/process

**Linked Lists v.s. Arrays: Data Management**

In general, if given the same data type to store in lists, arrays take less memory/storage space than linked lists. You'll find out about this later, but linked lists generally need slightly more data in its structure than arrays. However, in lists with very high number of items, this slight difference is actually significant.

# Chapter 12b: Linked Lists

The concept of linked lists is actually very simple.

Think of linked lists as a chain - literally. In a linked list, each "link" in the chain will have its item, followed by whatever "link" is next. If a certain link has no links next, then that link is at the end of the chain - or rather, the end of the linked list.

Here's an example of what a doubly linked list would look like visually:

[ ID01 ][ item ][ Prev: NULL][ Next: ID03]

[ ID04 ][ item ][ Prev: ID03][ Next: NULL]

[ ID03 ][ item ][ Prev: ID01][ Next: ID04]

There are three "links" in the chain, with link ID04 being the last one. Why is ID04 last? Easy - because there is no link after it.

And note how the IDs go from 01, then 04, and 03, and they're not in order. However, in linked lists, the numbers DO NOT tell you the order. I REPEAT. The NUMBERS DO NOT tell you the order

It's because    of one crucial fact about how the ordering in linked lists are set up.

*"The Ordering of a Linked List is this: The very first node (no nodes before it), then its next one, then the next one, and so on - until there's a node with nothing after it."*

**Building Linked Lists From Scratch:**

If you ever had to design a linked list from scratch, the concept is simple. A single link in a linked list consists of the actual data, then the ID of whatever the next or previous nodes are. Singly linked list nodes only point to the next node, while Doubly Linked List nodes point to both next and previous nodes.

In our pseudocode below, there are four key fields in a doubly linked list node: the ID, the previous node's ID, the next node's ID, and the actual data item.

*// Abstract Data Type: Linked List*

*// Each element in the Linked List is represented by a Node.*
*// A Node has:*
*// - an ID (String)*
*// - the ID of the Previous Node (String)*
*// - the ID of the Next Node (String)*
*// - the Data Item (choose what data type you want)*
*CompositeStructure Node {*
*String ID*
*String PREVID*
*String NEXTID*
*(choose a data type) ITEM*
*}*

Usually, you can only use one data type per each linked list. The reason is simply how the computer system itself processes and organizes data (you'll learn more about this if you know how Computer Systems themselves work).

# Chapter 12c: Arrays

If you look up the word 'array' in the dictionary, you'll find out that it's an elaborate, and sometimes beautiful, arrangement of items in a particular order.

Emphasize the phrase "arrangement of items in a particular order".

And in programming, you now know the key point of Arrays - they're a list of data items sorted in a particular order.

Here's an example of what an array with a size of 5 would look like visually:

[ 0 ][item A]

[ 1 ][item B]

[ 2 ][ NULL ]

[ 3 ][item D]

[ 4 ][ NULL ]

Here, you can see how quickly and easily you can add or get data items from an array. If you know the index where you stored your data, just access the array, the index, then the data is yours.

Also, arrays sizes are usually fixed. In some programming languages, there are also Dynamic or Variable-Size Arrays. But depending on how the programming language works, the data items are usually re-added into arrays that have as much room as the number of items.

**Quick Note: Why is Zero first?**

In Computer Science, data is counted from zero first. Meaning, 0 will be the first thing, 1 will be the second, 2 will be the third, and so on.

If it sounds confusing to you, just keep in mind that if you had to count within computer terms, have the i-th position in mind, minus one.

So if we had an array of 10 items, the very first item in the array would be in Index 0 (1st - 1) and the very last item in the list would be Index n - 1 (meaning, the size of your array, minus one.

**Building Arrays From Scratch:**

If you ever had to design a data array from scratch, the concept is simple too. But unlike linked lists, there aren't any individual nodes. Building an array requires two main things: the length or size of the array and the data type you want to store in it.

Most programming languages should be able to support simple arrays. In pseudocode, we create an array like so:

```
// Abstract Data Type: Array
// An Array has:
// - an Array Size
// - the Type of Data Item to Store (choose what
data type you want)
(choose a data type) ArrayName[ArraySize]
```

And just like linked lists, you can only use one data type per each array. Unlike linked lists, however, arrays are strict about having only one data type per array. The reason for this is how the computer assigns data memory/storage for that array. Having one data type per each array makes the array much more structured and easy to access.

# SWIFT-06: Linked Lists & Arrays in Swift

### Creating Arrays

Arrays in Swift are declared in the following format:

var <Variable Name> = [ <Data Type> ]()

In Swift, you also have the option to define your Array Size and Initial Values, respectively, via count and repeatedValue:

var <Variable Name> = [<Data Type>](count: ___ , repeatedValue: ___ )

To set up an array in Swift, use either line of code above. Then choose your variable name,and how many item objects you want in the array.

Here's an example. I'm declaring an array named 'intArray'. It will also have 10 integers initialized to 0 within it:

*var intArray = [Int](count: 10, repeatedValue: 0)*

## Accessing Array Items

You can access data objects within an array by calling the variable name, followed by its index (position within the array) as an integer within brackets:

<Variable Name>[ <index of array data object> ]

For example, if you wanted to access the third item in intArray, you would use this expression:

*... = intArray[2]*

But why 2 and not 3?

Because, remember, in Computer Science, data is counted from zero first!

## Creating Linked Lists from Scratch

This can be a little more tricky than usual, as you'll usually need to design a single node first.

Just remember what a Linked List node essentially consists of. For Singly Linked Lists, you'll need its contained data item and what the next node will be.

Here's the comments to design it:

```
// Abstract Data Type: Linked List, Singly
// Each element in the Linked List is represented by
a Node.
// A Node has:
// - the Data Item (choose what data type you want)
// - the Next Node (Node Object)
```

As for Doubly Linked Lists, you'll need the data item, as well as the previous and next nodes:

```
// Abstract Data Type: Linked List, Doubly
// Each element in the Linked List is represented by
a Node.
// A Node has:
// - the Data Item (choose what data type you want)
// - the Previous Node (Node Object)
// - the Next Node (Node Object)
```

# Chapter 13: Self-Reference Recursion

Self-Reference recursion - self-recursion for short - is one of the most important concepts in Computer Programming.

The main idea behind Self-Recursion is this: given some initial input, a self-recursive function will process an effect, then continue to repeat processing that effect with a reduced or augmented version of that input. The function will continue repeating its process - until the input is at a certain state that causes the function to stop repeating.

Self-reference is a key procedure in processing collections of data items. Given, a self-recursive function will repeat its procedure for each data item in the collection. The function will keep repeating until either there are no more data items left to process, or the function has encountered its intended solution.

This concept is seen throughout simple and advanced programming - including algorithms, auto-generating data, and more.

**Parts of the Self-Recursive Function**

Let's observe a Self-Recursive Function example in Pseudocode:

```
// INPUT: an Integer
// OUTPUT: none
// EFFECT: Given a positive integer, prints
10^(input),
// then repeats with input - 1 until it prints just 10
// - Base Case: input is <= 0
// - Recursive Step: Repeat with input - 1
void printPowerTen(integer i) {
        //Base Case:
        if (i <=0) return;

        // Recursive Step:
        print 10 ^ i;
        printPowerTen(i - 1); // this is the self-
reference
}
```

(remember: this concept will remain the same throughout many programming languages!)

A Self-Recursion function will have the main components of a regular function: possible inputs and outputs, and an effect.

It will also have two additional components: a Base Case and a Recursive Step.

To check whether or not the function has reached its base case, note its use of the IF statement above: As a condition, it checks whether or not the input has reached the base case. If true, the function returns and ends.

**Implementing the Function: The Base Case**

A Base Case is always the first component of a Self-Recursive Function.

You need to set your self-recursive function limit. This could be when either there are no more data items left to process or some variable or input is at a minimum/maximum value. Once your self-recursive function encounters that limit, the function should stop repeating and end.

In the example above, the base case is set when the input is not a positive integer - essentially when it's 0 or below. Whenever that becomes the function input, the function will return and end.

*// - Base Case: input is <= 0*

...

> *//Base Case:*
> *if (i <=0) return;*

Also, observe carefully. Remember the IF statements we went over in a previous chapter? Self-recursive functions will utilize that concept to check for the Base Case.

## Why you NEED a Base Case

Without a proper base case, a self-recursive function will process forever - a term called an Infinite Loop. The function will keep repeating its process despite having a reduced or augmented input. It wouldn't know how to stop processing, so it would go on forever.

" Eat, sleep, rave, repeat "

" Eat, sleep, rave, repeat "

" Eat, sleep, rave, repeat " ... and so on

**The Recursive Step: Self-Reference**

There are two main components in the Recursive Step: the function effect and the call to same function. That function call needs to have an input that steps closer to the Base Case.

Just as a typical function, the effect is whatever you've intended your function to do.

The call to the same function is what defines this as a Self-Recursive function. Note that in the last line of the example, there is a call to that same function. However, and most importantly, the input in that function is decremented by 1. And it's eventually going to be decremented all the way to 0 - the Base Case!

```
// - Recursive Step: Repeat with input - 1
...
     // Recursive Step:
     print 10 ^ i;
     printPowerTen(i - 1); // this is the self-
reference
...
```

## Tail-Recursive

A Self-reference Function is tail recursive when the very last line of its procedure is a call to itself. You want your self-recursive functions to have this; it helps ensure your function process the way you intend it to be.

In our example, the function is definitely self-recursive. There is a process to increment the input by one, then the function repeats itself using that input.

*printPowerTen(i - 1); // this is the self-reference*

## The Recursive Rule of thumb: TRUST THE RECURSION

You've defined what your function limit is. It's on your Base Case.

Now as long as your self-reference function is tail recursive, and the recursive function call's input is changed to a step closer to the base case, then your function should operate repeatedly over and over until it reaches a base case.

As long as you have these pieces in place, your recursive function should process as planned. You just need to Trust the Recursion.

Get your base case defined, call the function recursively, and set that input to inch closer to the base case.

## Defining the Function

While the function input and output will vary for each situation, the effect will remain consistent: the function will keep repeating and producing its desired effect until it hits its base case limit.

```
// INPUT: _____
// OUTPUT: _____
// EFFECT: _____
// - Base Case: function has reached a limit
// - Recursive Step: variable/input, with a step closer to reaching limit
```

Here's an example:

```
// INPUT: - Array of Strings, and a String Length
(Integer)
// OUTPUT: - Array of Strings
// EFFECT: Returns an array of Strings that have
the given string length
// - Base Case: function has no more Array
Elements to process
// - Recursive Step: Repeat without recently
processed String
Array[String] matchLength(Array[String]
stringArray, Integer length) {
    ...
}
```

# Chapter 14: Iteration Loops

Once you understand how recursive functions work, you'll understand how similar the next two chapters (iteration and while loops) are to self-recursion.

In essence, self-recursion, iteration loops, and while-loops have the same concept: repeat a process over and over, with each repeat a step closer to reaching some limit, then stop repeating and move on.

Self-Recursion, Iteration Loop, and While Loop functions will almost always involve some data collection, integer, or some number.

### Parts of the For-Loop Function

Let's observe a for-loop Function example in Pseudocode:

```
// INPUT: an Integer
// OUTPUT: none
// EFFECT: Given a positive integer, prints (input),
// then repeats and prints input - 1, then afterwards
// prints "WE HAVE LIFT OFF"
// - Start: given input
// - Continue: counting integer is > 0
```

```
// - Repeating Step: Repeat with input - 1
void printCountdown(integer input) {
        // this is the for-loop
        for (integer i = input; i > 0; input—) {

        //this is the looped procedure
        print(i);
        }

        // this occurs after the for-loop ends
        print("WE HAVE LIFT OFF")
}
```

(remember: this concept will remain the same throughout many programming languages!)

A for-loop function will also have the main components of a regular function: possible inputs and outputs, and an effect.

It will also have the three key components in an iteration loop: the start value, the continuing condition, and the next step. These describe how the loop will iterate and repeat a process.

How? The for-loop will use a counting integer, set it to the start value, process the looped procedure, then modify the counting integer. The for-loop will repeat the looped procedure over and over until the counting integer is at a certain value - a point where the continuing condition decides to stop.

**The Iteration's Start & Ends**

First, use an integer and give it a starting value - say, zero.

Next, define what the integer value should be in order to continue repeating: the continuing condition

*// - Start: 0*
*// - Continue: counting integer < given input*
*...*
    *// this is the for-loop*
    *for (integer i = 0; input > i; ... ) {*

You can also have your iteration loop inversely; the starting value as some integer and the continuing condition as the counting integer greater than 0.

*// - Start: given input*
*// - Continue: input is > 0*
*...*
    *// this is the for-loop*
    *for (integer i = input; i > 0; ... ) {*

## The Iteration's Next Step

Regardless, of what the start value and continuing condition should be, the next-step should change the counting integer value. Increment or decrement the integer to inch closer to disabling the continuing condition.

```
// - Repeating Step: Repeat with input - 1
...
        // this is the for-loop
        for ( ...              input—) {
```

This is comparable to the self-reference function call in the previous chapter. The for-loop will repeat the process within that loop, then change the counting integer.

It then repeats until the counting integer eventually causes the continuing condition to no longer repeat.


## Defining the Function, Inputs & Outputs

The function input and output varies, depending on the situation. However, the effect will remain consistent: the function will keep iterating and producing its desired effect until it hits its base case limit.

There are two commonly used versions, depending on how the iterating components are configured.

```
// Iterating Up
// INPUT: _____
// OUTPUT: _____
// EFFECT: _____
// - Start: 0
// - Continue: (set a limit) > counting integer
// - Repeating Step: (counting integer +1)
```

```
// Iterating Down
// INPUT: _____
// OUTPUT: _____
// EFFECT: _____
// - Start: (set a starting value)
// - Continue: 0 < counting integer
// - Repeating Step: (counting integer -1)
```

Using the array below, here's an example for each version, in pseudocode:

```
// an Array of Names (Strings)
String theArray[4] = ["Anna", "Betty", "Cammy", "Daphne"]
```

```
// Iterating Up
```

```
// INPUT: - none
// OUTPUT: - none
// EFFECT: print each name in the array, starting
with the first
// - Start: 0
// - Continue: (set a limit) > counting integer
// - Repeating Step: (counting integer +1)
void printArrayFromStart() {
        // this is the for-loop
        for (integer i = 0; 4 > i; i++) {
        print theArray[i]; // this will print
whatever's in the i-th position
        }
}


// Iterating Down
// INPUT: - none
// OUTPUT: - none
// EFFECT: print each name in the array, starting
with the last
// - Start: (set a starting value)
// - Continue: 0 < counting integer
// - Repeating Step: (counting integer -1)
void printArrayFromEnd() {
        // this is the for-loop
        for (integer i = 4; 0 < i; i—) {
        print theArray[i]; // this will print
whatever's in the i-th position
        }
}
```

Each version will go through the array in different directions. These directions depend on iteration parts: one will iterate from 0 to the array size, the other will iterate the opposite direction.

# Chapter 15: Iterations: While-Loops

Simply put, a While-loop is a more simple form of iteration.

It contains similar features to an IF-statement: it contains a repeat-condition (as a boolean statement), and a code to repeatedly process as long as that repeat-condition remains TRUE.

However, the repeating code within a While-Loop will keep repeating until the repeat-condition returns FALSE. Then, the code will move on.

And remember this concept: repeat a process over and over, with each repeat a step closer to reaching some limit, then stop repeating and move on. This is also true for the While-Loop.

Within the repeating code, there should be a line or two that changes the repeat-condition. It should be moved CLOSER to return FALSE, so that the while-loop will eventually stop repeating.

And just like the other iterative forms, a While-Loop function will almost always involve some data collection, integer, or some number. It needs this data for the repeat-condition. The data will be checked and the repeat-condition will either return TRUE or FALSE - therefore either repeating the code, or moving on.

In pseudocode, here's an example function that uses a While-Loop:

```
// INPUT: _____
// OUTPUT: _____
// EFFECT: _____
// - Repeat if: counting integer < (set a limit)
void countTo(Integer n){
        Integer LOCALCOUNTER = 0
        while (LOCALCOUNTER < n) {
        print(LOCALCOUNTER)
        LOCALCOUNTER++
        }
}
```

Now, let's analyze the While-Loop and its components:

**The Repeat-Condition**

The Repeating Code will be processed and continue to be re-processed as long as the Repeat-Condition remains true. In this example, a local variable integer will initially be set to 0. As long as the local variable is less than the limit (the Input Integer), the while-loop will repeat.

*...*
*// - Repeat if: counting integer < (set a limit)*
*...*
*while (LOCALCOUNTER < n) {*
*....*

## The Repeating Code

As you can guess, this portion of the code will keep repeating as long as the Repeat-Condition is TRUE.

However, there has to be at least ONE line of code that makes the next repetitions inch CLOSER to the Repeat-Condition to be FALSE - hence, stop repeating.

Note the example. The counting integer is incremented during every repetition. Eventually, that counting integer will be equal to or larger than the limit - hence, the function will stop repeating.

...

```
while (LOCALCOUNTER < n) {
print(LOCALCOUNTER)
LOCALCOUNTER++
}
```

...

**Again, TRUST THE RECURSION!**

At heart, a while-loop will almost always be a self-recursive function (figuratively speaking).

Just make sure your repeat-condition will have some sort of limit, and your repeating code will inch closer to that limit. And eventually, your function will keep repeating and repeating until a certain point, then move on.

Again, as long as you have these pieces in place, your while-loop function should process as planned. You just need to Trust the Recursion.

# SWIFT-07a: Iteration in Swift

In any programming language, Self-Recursion and Iteration are your best tools for processing through entire lists of data objects.

Why? Think about it for a second.

If you have a list of data elements, and you need to process every single element in that list, wouldn't that mean having to repeat the same function for each data element?

Hence, that's why you'll need these concepts to go through lists.

Let's run through an example, with this list below:

*// STR_ARRAY is an array of Strings, with 5 slots*
*var STR_ARRAY = [String](count: 5, repeatedValue: "")*

Now, say you entered five of your best friends onto that list:

*STR_ARRAY[0] = "Amy"*
*STR_ARRAY[1] = "Ben"*

*STR_ARRAY[2] = "Charlie"*
*STR_ARRAY[3] = "Diana"*
*STR_ARRAY[4] = "Emily"   ;*

So what if we wanted to identically modify each element in this array? Or what if we wanted to identically process them?

You guessed it. Self-Recursion or Iteration!

Let's make a function. It will print each item in the array after adding a string.

```
// INPUT: - a String Array
// OUTPUT: - none
    // EFFECT: - Prints every String in the array
along with an additional string
func addPrint(array: [String], addString: String)-
>Void {
    // How should we implement this?????
}
```

You can try this out too. Copy-paste each function stub within your Swift code.

We're also going to add function calls after you've set your friends' names. So it would look like so:

```
STR_ARRAY[0] = "Amy"
STR_ARRAY[1] = "Ben"
STR_ARRAY[2] = "Charlie"
STR_ARRAY[3] = "Diana"
STR_ARRAY[4] = "Emily"
addPrint(STR_ARRAY, "Is My Friend!")
```

Copy-paste the above to your Swift code, just after the Function declarations.

Afterwards, you'll run your code. But of course nothing happens because you haven't implemented the working functionality within function adddPrint() yet!

But using comments, we've established what we've wanted our functions to do. So if you run the final code, this should print:

*Amy Is My Friend!*
*Ben Is My Friend!*
*Charlie Is My Friend!*
*Diana Is My Friend!*
*Emily Is My Friend!*

So let's start getting our functions to work.

We'll start by using For-Loops and While-Loops.

**For-Loop Iteration for an Array**

What would you initially set the iterator to?

What number can the iterator be to keep repeating?

And how would you modify the iterator to stop repeating the function?

Think carefully about how you would iterate through the list and modify each element. Remember what we want in our comments; we want to add a String to each array element.

However, note that we can access each array element using its index. And each element in the list is going to be indexed from 0 to the array size.

Therefore, we can iterate from 0 to the array size! And we can modify each element using its index!

So we've figured out how we're going to iterate the functionality. For aMod(), let's set the iterator from 0 to the item size.

Here's the function so far:

```
// INPUT: - a String Array
// OUTPUT: - none
    // EFFECT: - Prints every String in the array
along with an additional string
// As a For-Loop:
// - Start: iterator at 0
// - Continue: iterator is less than array size
// - Repeating Step: iterator + 1
    func addPrint(var array: [String], addString:
String)->Void {
    for var i = 0; i < array.count; i++ {
        // ???
    }
}
```

But what will the functionality be? Well, we know what we want. Let's just use our operator:

```
// INPUT: - a String Array
// OUTPUT: - none
    // EFFECT: - Prints every String in the array
along with an additional string
```

```
// As a For-Loop:
// - Start: iterator at 0
// - Continue: iterator is less than array size
// - Repeating Step: iterator + 1
    func addPrint(var array: [String], addString:
String)->Void {
    for var i = 0; i < array.count; i++ {
      array[i] += " " + addString
      println(array[i])
    }
}
```

And there we go!

Try out the code and see if it adds and prints each array element properly!

**While-Loop Iteration for an Array**

We can also have the same result by setting up each function as a While-Loop iteration.

But how do we do this? Let's think about it.

For our Repeating Condition, we just want to keep repeating the same functionality for all the elements in the array - until there's no more elements to repeat the functionality for.

Since we're dealing with an array, we can access each data element using their indices. Since array indices are integers, we can use a counting integer to iterate through the array. So We can repeat the functionality from 0 to the array size - just as if we were using a For-Loop!

```
// INPUT: - a String Array
// OUTPUT: - none
    // EFFECT: - Prints every String in the array
along with an additional string
// As a While-Loop:
// - Set up a counting integer & init at 0
// - Repeat if: counting integer < array size
    func addPrint(var array: [String], addString:
String)->Void {
  var i = 0;
      while (i < b.length) {
      // ???
      i++;
  };
```

We've already managed to figure out the repeating functionality from the For-Loop version. So here's the function:

```
func addPrint(var array: [String], addString:
String)->Void {
  var i = 0
  while i < array.count {
    array[i] += " " + addString
    println(array[i])
    i++
  }
}
```

Try out the code and see if it adds and prints each array element properly!

# SWIFT-07b: Self-Recursion in Swift

For linked lists, your best tools for processing through each list is self-recursion.

But why not for-loops? Because a For-Loop uses an integer to iterate through the array - from end to end. Arrays have indices for functions and methods to iterate through. But Linked Lists don't.

Instead, for Linked Lists, you can repeat the functionality over and over for the rest of the Linked Lists - until you've reached the end of the Linked List (your Base Case!)

From the last chapter, what if your list of names were a linked list instead? Below is what it would look like.

In Swift, here's a Singly Linked List Node Class, along with your same 5 best friends included into a Linked List. Copy-paste it to your code like so:

*// Abstract Data Type: Linked List, Singly*

```
// Each element in the Linked List is represented by
a Node.
// A Node has:
// - the Data Item (choose what data type you want)
// - the Next Node (Node Object)
class Node {
   var data = ""
   var next: Node!
   init() {


   }
}


// INPUT: - a String Array
// OUTPUT: - none
// EFFECT: - Adds a String to linked list node until
end of list
func aMod(node: Node!, stringToAdd: String) {
   if let n = node {
      var x = node.data + " " + stringToAdd
      node.data = x
      aMod(node.next, stringToAdd)}
   else {
      return
   }
}


// INPUT: - a String Array
```

```
// OUTPUT: - none
// EFFECT: - Prints every String in the Linked List
Input
func aPrint(node: Node!) {
    if let n = node {
        println(node.data)
        aPrint(node.next)}
    else {
        return
    }
}


var a = Node()
a.data = "Amy"
a.next = nil
var b = Node()
b.data = "Ben"
b.next = a
var c = Node()
c.data = "Charlie"
c.next = b
var d = Node()
d.data = "Diana"
d.next = c
var e = Node()
e.data = "Emily"
e.next = d
```

```
aMod(e, "is my Friend!");
aPrint(e);

  }
}
```

Now, let's implement the functionality for both aMod() and aPrint() - so that running the code above will print out this:

*Emily is my Friend!*
*Diana is my Friend!*
*Charlie is my Friend!*
*Ben is my Friend!*
*Amy is my Friend!*


## Self-Reference Recursion for a Linked List

So we're going to implement the two functions using Self-Recursion.

Think about what a Linked List consists of: a group of Linked Nodes. You'll repeat the function for each Linked List node. But eventually, you'll end up reaching the end of the Linked List. And how do you know if you did? Easy. What if you found a node with nothing next to it - in this case, what if the next node is null?

And there's your functionality's limit - or in other words, the Base Case. You can end your function if there's no more nodes to iterate through.

```
// INPUT: - a String Array
// OUTPUT: - none
    // EFFECT: - Adds String c to every String in
array b
// As Self-Reference:
// - Base Case: input is null (end of list)
// - Recursive Step: Repeat for Next Node
func aMod(node: Node!, stringToAdd: String) {
    // ???
};
```

Now, let's start writing the code.

Recall that you need your Base Case, Recursive Step, and your actual Functionality:

```
func aMod(node: Node!, stringToAdd: String) {
    // Base Case:
    // ???
    // Recursive Step:
    else {
        // ???
```

```
    // ???
  }
};
```

We know what we need for the Base Case; if you've reached the end of the list (if your input is null), end the functionality. For the Recursive Step, repeat the function for the NEXT node in the list. And for the Main Functionality, we know what we want - based on the comments we wrote.

(NOTE: In Swift, because of how null-checking works, the Base Case is actually on the ELSE part of the statement - not the IF!)

```
func aMod(node: Node!, stringToAdd: String) {

    // Recursive Step:
    if let n = node {
    var x = node.data + " " + stringToAdd
    node.data = x
    aMod(node.next, stringToAdd)}
    // Base Case:
    else {
    return
  }
```

```
};
```

Let's also finish aPrint() using the same concepts:

(NOTE: Remember, the Base Case is actually on the ELSE part of the statement - not the IF!)

```
// INPUT: - a String Array
// OUTPUT: - none
// EFFECT: - Prints every String in the Linked List
Input
    // As Self-Reference:
    // - Base Case: input is null (end of list)
    // - Recursive Step: Repeat for Next Node
func aPrint(node: Node!) {
        // Recursive Step:
    if let n = node {
        println(node.data)
        aPrint(node.next)}
      // Base Case:
    else {
        return
    }
}
```

Now after you've implemented the functions, try running it and see if you've printed the right output.

And remember: Trust the Recursion!

# PART V: Special Data Structures

# Chapter 16: Binary Trees

Think of your family tree - with just you, both your parents, all your grandparents, great grandparents, and so on.

You'll quickly realize that there's one of you, there's up to two of your parents, up to four of your grandparents, up to eight of your great-grandparents, and so on.

And if you were to lay everyone out on a chart - with you at the top, your parents at the next row, then your grandparents on the next row, and so on - it would look like a 'tree'.

In this case, it would look like a Binary Tree: a single node would have two 'sub-nodes', and each of those sub-nodes would have two sub-nodes, and those sub-nodes would have their own sub-nodes, and so on.

Overall, a Binary tree structure would look like this:

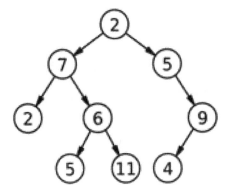

**What Binary Trees are for**

Tree structures, in general, are one of the most important data structures for computing. This is especially true for search & answer-generator algorithms - even auto-sentence completion.

Binary trees, in particular, are one of the simpler tree structures for computing. The data is laid out in such as way that a recursive algorithm can process each node and both its child-nodes. Sometimes, using a binary tree and its algorithm on a list may process that list FASTER than simply iterating through that whole list!

To give you an idea of how binary trees work, here's an example.

I'm thinking of a random number between 1 and 100. If you guess what number it is, I'll either tell you to guess higher, lower, or that you've got the answer. So if you were to say 50, I'll either tell you higher or lower (it's not 50; so keep guessing), then you'd guess again, then I'll tell you higher or lower, and so on until you've got the answer.

How would you figure out what the number is?

More importantly, how would you use a Binary tree structure & algorithm to figure out what number it is?

Well, you know the data will be laid out as a binary tree. So you know you'll need a matching algorithm to process it. If I pick my number for you to guess, you would run your algorithm - which would randomly choose a number and check that number against mine. Then your algorithm's number will either be the correct number or not. If it's not, your algorithm's number will either be higher or lower than mine. Your algorithm would then choose another number closer to my number and repeat the process - over and over until it guesses my number correctly!

Ultimately, you wouldn't even have to solve it yourself - a computer program can do it for you.

### Simple Binary Tree Rules

At the core minimum, a valid Binary tree should have the following:

- each tree node represents some amount of data: atomic or compound data will do

- each node should have up to two sub-nodes: a left and/or right sub-node

- if a node has no sub-nodes, it's called a Leaf node

There are many different subtypes of binary trees, each with its own set of additional structure rules. For example: there are Binary Search Trees, Minimum Heaps, Maximum Heaps, AVL Trees, and more.

## The Data Structure

For each node in a binary tree, it will either have left/right sub-nodes nodes, or have no nodes at all (these are called leaf nodes).

Here is some general pseudocode below. You can implement your Binary Tree node on any programming language you wish, depending on what you need to be done.

```
// A Binary Tree Node contains:
// - a data key (whatever data type you want)
// - a Left Sub-Node (either a BTreeNode or NULL)
// - a Right Sub-Node (either a BTreeNode or NULL)
CompositeStructure BTreeNode {
<data type of your choice> key
BTreeNode LEFT
BTreeNode RIGHT
}
```

### General Processing Function:

If you've read this far, you may have gone over self-recursive functions already (if not, you may want to go back and quickly skim through). The general function resembles a self-recursive function, with a base case and two self-recursive calls for both left and right sub-nodes.

The general algorithm for processing a Binary Tree is below:

```
// INPUT: - a Binary Tree Node
// OUTPUT: - <choose your output data type>
// EFFECT: _____
// - Base Case: input is NULL
// - Recursive Steps: recursive call to left & right
sub-trees
<chosen output data type> procBTree(BTreeNode n)
{
        // BASE CASE:
        if (n == NULL) {
        return <chosen output data type>
        }

        // MAIN PROC:
        // whatever code you want here

        // RECURSIVE CALL: LEFT TREE
        procBTree(n-LEFT)
```

*// RECURSIVE CALL: RIGHT TREE*
*procBTree(n-LEFT)*

*}*

## The Inputs:

The input will almost always be a node.

*// INPUT: - a Binary Tree Node*
*...*
*... procBTree(BTreeNode n) {*
*...*

## The Base Case

Most binary tree algorithms will repeat processing until there's no node remaining to process. At this point, the function will return (possibly with a data type you've set) and not self-recurse for any sub-nodes.

> *// BASE CASE:*
> *if (n == NULL) {*
> *return <chosen output data type>*
> *}*

## The Recursive Step

Just like a self-recursive function, a binary tree algorithm will repeat itself for both sub-nodes (and sub-trees). These lines of code will be one more step closer to reaching your base case - no nodes.

> *// RECURSIVE CALL: LEFT TREE*
> *procBTree(n-LEFT)*
> *// RECURSIVE CALL: RIGHT TREE*
> *procBTree(n-LEFT)*

## Remembering the Recursive Rule: TRUST THE RECURSION

We've gone over this before in the Self-Recursion chapter. Just make sure your function has a limit and each self-recursive function call is a step closer to that limit. Then you just need to trust the recursion and let it run.

For Binary Trees, as long as your function has a point where it will stop processing (your base case: a NULL node), and your function's self-recursive call processes both left and right sub-nodes, your code will run. Just like the above, you need to trust the recursion.

## Last Words

Thank you again for purchasing this book!

I hope this book was able to help you.

The next step is to apply what you've learned.

Finally, if you enjoyed this book, please take the time to share your thoughts and post a review on Amazon. It'd be greatly appreciated!

www.ingramcontent.com/pod-product-compliance
Lightning Source LLC
Chambersburg PA
CBHW031219050326
40689CB00009B/1396